Whispers *and* Wailings

Whispers *and* Wailings

Untold Stories of
Migrant Workers in the Middle East

KHAN R. MOSLEH

Whispers and Wailings

Copyright 2021 © Khan Mosleh

All information, techniques, ideas and concepts contained within this publication are of the nature of general comment only and are not in any way recommended as individual advice. The intent is to offer a variety of information to provide a wider range of choices now and in the future, recognizing that we all have widely diverse circumstances and viewpoints. Should any reader choose to make use of the information contained herein, this is their decision, and the contributors (and their companies), authors and publishers do not assume any responsibilities whatsoever under any condition or circumstances. It is recommended that the reader obtain their own independent advice.

First Edition 2021

ISBN: 978-1-7376170-1-3

All rights reserved in all media. No part of this book may be used, copied, reproduced, presented, stored, communicated or transmitted in any form by any means without prior written permission, except in the case of brief quotations embodied in critical articles and reviews.

The moral right of Khan Mosleh as the author of this work has been asserted by him in accordance with the Copyrights, Designs and Patents Act of 1988.

Published by Happy Self Publishing
www.happyselfpublishing.com

Index

Testimonials..*vii*
About Whispers and Wailings ....*ix*

Chapters

1 A Drama and Few Agonies 1
2 Humanity vs. Inhumanity 7
3 Misconception About the Middle East......................................17
4 The Horrible Incident at Holy Artisan 23
5 Bangladesh: Then and Now 27
6 UAE: The Country in Detail...33
7 Moving to Villas and Meeting Hossein....................................41
8 The Exploitation of Migrant workers 53
9 A Shocking Incident and UAE Visa Ban for Bangladeshi Workers 57
10 Facts of Islamic Beliefs..65
11 The Caged Birds..71
12 Hossein's Daily Life..77
13 Living Conditions of Migrant Workers....................................83

14	Story of 49 Workers and Bangladeshi Consulate	91
15	The Contribution of Middle Eastern Workers to the National Economy	97
16	The Hypocrisy of the Bangladeshi Elite Class	111
17	Eid-ul-Adha	117
18	An Unfortunate Bangladeshi Girl	127
19	My Departure	135
20	Qatar	143
21	Job in the Middle East: All You Need to Know	147
22	Seven Deadly Sins	153
23	My Motivational Speech	163

Acknowledgments *169*
Thank You *173*
About Happy Self Publishing *175*

Testimonials

I have been to the Middle East many times and have witnessed the arduous lives of the Bengali workers. Mr. Khan has captured their plight and their undying spirit with complete accuracy.

Col. Dr. James Cummings

What a read! Beautifully written. The author shares his real-life experiences. Mosleh Khan has done it with a finesse that only a talented author like him possibly could. A MUST read.

Dilano Burah

This is a really fantastic book. It represents not only Khan's life but also the contemporary situation of that time.

Labonne Poddar

We hope to see more literary genius works from you in years to come, adding to Bengali literature!

Mo Haque

This book is beautifully written. It has a very remarkable story, which at the beginning, is a little emotional. May Allah guide the man who has written this book.

Moklesur Rahman

About Whispers and Wailings

I have been a passionate reader since childhood, so quoting that I have read piles of books would not be an overstatement. So far, I have read books in several fiction and non-fiction genres. And now, I can say beyond any reasonable doubt that I have been an ultra-focused reader. While reading books by famous authors, I have always dreamt of bringing my own book to the daylight. From my college life, when I was in Bangladesh, I felt an urge to write, touching many burning issues. However, during my sophomore years at Dhaka University, I got an opportunity to switch over to an American university and moved to the US afterward. Now, I have been living in the US for almost four decades. During the course, I worked for several companies, ventured into some businesses. Eventually, I landed in a position that endowed me the opportunity to teach for the University of Maryland Global Campus, an American University with branches in different countries in the World.

Although I initially started writing *Whispers and Wailings* on the Bangladeshi labors' untold struggles in the Middle East, but my first published book turned out to be an *Atmaprokash (Self-Revelation)*. As *Whispers and Wailings* have been a continuous process, so I decided to write a book based on my memories. I began to write by incorporating the assets of my remembrances, which I harvested during my two-year stay at Dhaka University, Bangladesh. Side by side, I wrote a few articles on some national and international issues that came up as exceptionally intriguing. Atmaprokash (Self-Revelation) is a compilation of those articles aligned chronologically and transformed into a book. I hope the readers enjoy those articles from the perspective of a candid, politically neutral, and bystander author. I received tons of encouragement from my friends and relatives in this venture, which I must recall with utmost gratitude.

Whispers and Wailings is research work. I have been living in different countries of the Middle East as a US citizen since January 1, 2012, for my job and university teaching. I have come in touch with thousands of Bangladeshi laborers in this long period and have been all ears to their heartbreaking stories. In Bangladesh, these laborers are entitled as 'the remittance warriors', but they are severely mistreated. And in the Middle East, they call these forsaken people 'Miskin' (beggar). These brave wage-earners work for 12 to 14 hours a day, six days a week, and some even work 29 days in a month only to keep their families content. In 2016, I came to know Hossein, a housekeeper at neighbors, and caught sight of his daily life. When I learned about his untold life story by observing him closely, I felt an obligation to write about him and other unprivileged hired hands to let the world know their heart-wrenching stories. Since then, I have been collecting stories from the workers, and the process is still on. In this book, I have also shared the social and geographical information about the Middle East to introduce the readers to this land. As I have got much appreciation regarding this research, therefore, I felt encouraged to write more.

The book has already been published in the Bengali language, and it's already widely accepted among Bangladeshi readers. An article containing all the necessary information that one may need to know about jobs in the Middle East is attached in the end. I dedicate this book to the millions of Bangladeshi workers in the Middle East. I believe that my hard work will pay off if this book creates even an iota of difference in someone's life.

Khan Mosleh

Chapter 1

A Drama and Few Agonies

"Sir, do you want to have some dates?", as I walked out, the boy who came running asked me this, his name is Hossain; the hero of my story. Hossein is not a fictional character; he is one of my acquaintances. It was the year 2016 when I met him in Abu Dhabi, United Arab Emirates (UAE). We will wade through the life of this unsung hero in the later chapters.

From time immemorial, Bangladesh's working-class people have fueled their economic wheel and set their family's condition in motion by sacrificing their happiness in foreign lands. This book is my small effort to take the wraps off their plight on foreign soil. They are primarily neglected people in their homeland, most of them being cut off from what they ironically call the 'Moddhoprachcher Kamla' (toiler of the Middle East). This situation arouses an uncanny feeling in me, as it reminds me of some native Bangladeshi lyrics, which I heard a long time ago but couldn't comprehend the full depth at that time. I am citing an example here:

"Listen, commoners
The ones who do not call humans
The rules do not comply with those who cry
They are also human who wail for their lives
I am singing for them with yowls."

Singer: Md. Abdul Jobbar
Lyrics: K. G. Mostofa
Tune: Anowar Uddin Khan

A few days back, I watched a YouTube drama, *Kalur Balad* (Miller's Bull), released in 2018. In this play, the playwright Mezbah Uddin Sumon and the Director Sajjad Sumon unveiled the social scenario regarding these Middle Eastern workers from Bangladesh. Many have agreed that it portrayed the real picture of their lives. More than ten thousand comments in the comment section on YouTube say that these workers are considered "gold egg-laying duck" back home. As long as they can provide gold eggs to their families, they are loved and appreciated. But when this stops, they lose value and indeed are dumped. In this regard, another song drops anchor on my mind:

"The wordless cries buried in their chests
No one understands, and no one listens
The pain of the hired-hands
People whose lives are built on sorrow, whose names are human
I am singing for them with tears in my eyes.
Life has been playing ceaseless sarcastic jokes with them
Nobody sees, nobody writes
Their history in this world
Those who sweat in the blistering dust of the road
I am singing for them with tears in my eyes."

Singer: Md. Abdul Jobbar
Lyrics: K. G. Mostofa
Composer: Anowar Uddin Khan

Some quotes in the comment section of the play *Kalur Balad* are worth reading as they are gut-wrenching. Here are some of the assertions:

Habib Allauddin wrote:

I was crying as long as I was watching the play. I spent at least ten years abroad and gave at least 40 lakh taka (4 million Bangladeshi currencies) (around 47,000 USD) to my family. I have a good job abroad; I work in a pharmacy. Today, I don't even know where the 40 lakh taka have gone. Even after that, the demands of the family never end. Today, I cry silently. I sent that 40 lakh taka in cash. Apart from that, I got married two years ago. I think I have spent another 10 lakh taka (around 11,600 USD) on the two trips for my own wedding, siblings' mobile phones, and ornaments. I am too tired, and I do not want to live in exile anymore. Today I am almost 33 years old. I am not the father of a child yet. I can't take it anymore. To whom should I tell this sorrow? I have spent all my life and youth in the 'prison with an invisible cage' called abroad. Now my tears are my only companion. Every woman wants her husband beside her to share happiness and sorrow after marriage, but I can't be by her side yet. I can't do that. Everyone, please pray for me. I am sorry to take a little more time. I have expressed my sorrow and lightened my mind a little.

Nizamuddin Sunny expressed:

An avalanche of tears is hidden in the minds of expatriates, and they cannot tell anyone. Even though I have tears in my eyes, I always smile and tell my family that I am happy when I call them.

Ashraful Islam wrote:

From the time I saw the play, I have cried rivers. I have been abroad for 12 long years. I have earned more than 5 million takas (around 58,000 USD), but I still can't get the family's attention. I can't write anything anymore; my eyes are brimful with tears. God bless you.

Mohammad Miraj wrote:

Hats off to him whoever wrote this play. It seems like everyone, including Riaz Bhai who acted in this drama, are all expatriates. Expatriates are never evaluated. On behalf of all expatriates, I think this drama deserves the Nobel Prize. Such a substantial role has been presented here that has coincided with 100% of expatriates' lives.

Awal wrote:

I have been trying to visit home for the last five years but unable to go. Every time, some or the other obstacle turns into a stone wall between me and my home back in Bangladesh. For numerous times, I planned to celebrate Eid in Bangladesh but every time, I end up greeting Eid to myself in the foreign land (Kuwait). Sometimes I feel so depressed that my pillow dampens with my tears but can't say anything to anybody.

Mansoor wrote:

I am an emigrant writing from Malaysia. No family member from Bangladesh ever inquired about my whereabouts. I am just sending money; no one asks me how I am or how much blood and sweat I have been putting in to earn every single ounce of that money. I watched the drama 'Kalur Balad'. It certainly reflects the lives of all emigrants. May Allah bless all expatriates, Amen.

In *Kalur Balad*, the playwright depicts the social mistreatment that the laborers face in Bangladesh. And this book is my small effort to bring out into the open how the same workers make hard-earned money by sweating out their heads across this side of the Arabian Sea. Here comes another song to say it right:

*"Friends, don't be sad
Tune in to that earlier melody
My song to pipe
Do not question, carry no arrogance in the heart.

The song that I lost
In the crowd of sad people,
The mourning sun lost in the darkness of sorrow
Many dreams vanish in the hope of failure."*

Artist: Abdul Jabbar
Lyricist: Mutafizur Rahman
Composer: Satya Saha

Chapter 2

Humanity vs. Inhumanity

A few days back, Ishtiyaque, a Bangladeshi young man, shared his tragic life story with me. He is from Chakbazar, Chottogram, a port city of Bangladesh. Ishtiyaque came to Qatar in December 2010 with the help of his friend's elder brother. Ishtiyaque didn't get any advantage as an acquaintance, though. He had to pay his friend's elder brother 20 thousand Riyal, which is more than 450 thousand in Bangladeshi currency (around 5200 USD).

The friend's elder brother works for the company. Sometimes the company needs an additional workforce. He managed to convince his boss to bring workers from Bangladesh. The company issued NOC (No Objection Certificate) for visa purposes to bring new employees. To issue NOC, the company or the boss do not charge any money. In most cases, the company bears all the expenses, because of their needs.

Ishtiyaque had to pay half of the amount before arriving in Qatar, and he paid the rest of the money by working hard after coming here. This friend's elder brother didn't give a single penny to his boss, he took it all. Besides, he has been charging money from many people like Ishtiyaque. That friend's elder brother has managed to build a big house in his hometown. Ishtiyaque even worked hard in building that house of his friend's brother to get a chance to come to Qatar. He told me that he has been living here (Qatar) for more than ten years and sends a big part of his salary to his family in Bangladesh every month. Ishtiyaque goes to Bangladesh with lots of gifts for his family members when he leaves for few days every two years. On all such visits, he bought some jewelry for his would-be wife and handed it over to his mother. But to his sheer surprise, he found out that the ornaments were missing when he went home a couple of years ago. His brothers and sisters took the possession considering those to be their mother's property, even though Ishtiyaque disbursed a considerable amount of money for their education and other pieces of stuff.

Ishtiyaque helped his nephew go abroad, but that boy couldn't live there for long as he could not tolerate the grind of hard work. Moreover, his sister, brother-in-law, and nephew planned to embezzle his money. I was amazed hearing the story of Ishtiyaque and suggested him to watch the drama "Kalur Balad" as I didn't know how to console that poor man.

Like Ishtiyaque, I have talked to a number of Bangladeshi workers so far, and most of them shared their stories of struggles with me. I felt deep compassion for them and thought that some of the stories must be listed for my readers.

Selim, who has been working like a Trojan for more than 11 years in this foreign land, told me a sad story. He spent a tremendous amount of money for his sister's wedding, but that sister has no concern for him; she doesn't even call him on any occasion like Eid (Muslim celebration). Many Eid days have passed, but that sister has never wished him. Selim sponsored his brother's business and bought him a car, but that brother also never talks to him. He got married four years ago but couldn't go home after that because he doesn't have enough money. He is 34 now and still has a dream of becoming a father, but who knows…? People like Selim want to catch the mirage in this desert and surviving with small hopes. Whatever they have bartered for their toil, sweat and blood; everything has leaked out to the drain called 'thankless', repelling them quarters away from the zone of peace.

"Dejected, all are crying bitterly,
Listen, O dear father.
Soothe souls, whisper into ears
All your right words.
Meager hopes they live with,
Everlasting anxieties,
Often lose whatever they earn,
Hard to console.
Wandering all over seeking glee,
Stagger hopeless,
Lunge to grab whatever they see,
Misinterpret illusions.
The game ends, time seems over
Night falls, slow,
Gloomy soul weeping anxiously,
Panic and trembles so.
What's in our fate, Universal King,

> *Where to find peace,*
> *Desires met when you offer yourself,*
> *Come closer, please."*
>
> **Rabindranath Tagore**
> **Written on: 1883**
> **Translation: Anjan Ganguli**
> **Collection: Robichhaya**

Khokon Molla is from Gopalganj, and he came to Qatar in 2014. Before landing in Qatar, he used to work in a knitwear factory in Bangladesh. He bought his Qatar visa for four and a half lakh taka (Bangladeshi currency) (around 5200 USD) with the help of Mr. Mojibor, who was Molla's landlord. Molla has been doing the job of a waiter in a Cafeteria for six years. He works seven days a week and only gets one or two days off in a month. When I asked him how long he wished to stay in Qatar, Molla answered that he aimed to gather one million takas (around 11,600 USD) for his son's job as he wanted his son to be a law enforcement officer. Once he gathers the said corpus, he would go back home. His aspiration piqued my curiosity as to why would he need so much money for that. That boy can easily get a job if he passes the entrance exam. Khokan Molla replied that his son wouldn't get the job if he doesn't pay enough money as a bribe. I was shocked to hear that.

Many laborers (at least 50 of them) have told me about this man named Mr. Mojibor. He helped lots of laborers in migrating to Qatar. In most cases, he took a minimal amount of money (in some cases, no money at all) to get them here. He also helped the laborers get jobs. Saddam, a young man from

Netrokona, Bangladesh, told me that he came to Qatar in 2014 with the help of Mr. Mojibor, and he did not have to pay at all. Saddam works at the company cafeteria as a waiter. Our company provides the cafeteria facility where the employees dine every day. Back in Dhaka, he also used to work at a sweater company. Haroon Khan from Nawabganj Dhaka and Bortholamoy Richil from Haluaghat, Mymensingh, also told me that they only paid for the airfare. They also came to Qatar with the help of Mr. Mojibor. I got an earful of similar stories from Akhtar, Khokon from Barishal, Halim from Comilla, and many more.

Mr. Mojibor works as a head of a branch at Tamimi Group of Company here in Qatar. Erstwhile, Tamimi Group suddenly needed a lot of workers because they got a massive contract from the USA government. Mr. Mojibor convinced his owner and managed lots of visas for the Bangladeshi workers. However, in the UAE, I did not find anyone so helpful as Mr. Mojibor; instead, I encountered quite the opposite. I even heard about another man (not revealing the name as the book does not intend to demean anyone until proven guilty) who made several millions of Taka's (hundreds of thousand USD) fortune by managing visas for Bangladeshi workers.

I never had the chance to meet Mr. Mojibur. However, those benefited boys will remember his name with respect for a long time. Throughout the ages, just as a generous-hearted person like Haji Muhammad Mohsin has been born in this country, so has a blood-sucking man like the Shailak character created by William Shakespeare. It isn't easy to understand where the scale is heavy in the present age. That is why the famous lyricist, composer, and musician Dr. Bhupen Hazarika has appealed to the world to sing the song of humanity:

"People are for people,
Life is for life
Can't people have some space for sympathy, O dear
Tell me, is it your loss if the weak
Hold your hand to cross the deep river.
If the man is not human
Monsters can never be kindhearted
If human turns into monsters
Won't you be ashamed, O dear?"

Dr. Bhupen Hazarika

Aminul from Gazipur was not much fortunate as he had to spend three lakh forty thousand takas (around 4,000 USD) to come to Qatar. Before arriving in Qatar, he was informed that would have to work for 8 hours a day in a high wash company, and he would get 800 Qatari Riyals (18,630 Bangladeshi Taka) (around 220 USD) per month. However, if he works 4 hours of overtime, he will get 400 riyals more, which means an additional 9315 taka (around 110 USD). He used to drive an auto-rickshaw in Bangladesh, and his family had to go through a lot of trouble to gather a tremendous amount of money. They only had one lakh taka (around 1,160 USD), and his parents had to borrow the remaining amount from different sources. Aminul's father used to run a small business, but he was bedridden for a long time due to illness. However, after coming to Qatar, Aminul found a significant discrepancy in the information given to him. He has to work for almost 13 hours per day, and not a single penny has been paid for overtime yet in these five years. His job is to seek the car owner's permission and clean at least 20 cars daily that come into the shopping center. Most car owners have their car washed by a housekeeper (we know that from Hossein). Due to the backbreaking effort and time, he usually falls short of the assigned target. Therefore, it takes extra two hours.

Moreover, in the Middle East, only the sufferers know how difficult it is to clean heated cars, one after another, for 12/13 hours in an open parking lot. The sweltering heat of 45 to 50 degrees Celsius (113 to 122 degrees Fahrenheit) is what adds insult to the injury. There is no chance to sit in the shade. Aminul's company employs about 1,000 workers, of whom about 600 are Bangladeshis; the remaining 400 are Nepalese, Sri Lankans, and Indians. Two owners (Azad and Javed) are from Jordan, and the manager is from Nepal. Out of 800 riyals (around 220 USD), 500 riyals (around 140 USD) go for accommodation and ancillary expenses; the remaining 300 riyals (6,740 Bangladeshi takas) (around 80 USD) can be sent to the country. In the case of Aminul, it costs 1,600 takas (around 20 USD) per month for the father's treatment, the remaining 5,000 takas (around 60 USD) is used to support the parents, wife, and daughter. But at times, some vehicle owners give him tips, but it's not a significant amount. If Aminul's employer knows about the tips, he must surrender that tips money to his owner. He is not allowed to keep any money that includes alms. I asked him how much money he used to earn by running an auto-rickshaw in the country. He said that even after paying the rickshaw owner's monthly rent, he would take home 10,000 takas (around 120 USD). Then he came to Qatar after spending a tremendous amount of money, and now regrets it. He wants to return to his home country as soon as the flight to Bangladesh starts in December (This is an estimated time based on the data available at the time of writing this book). Aviation is currently closed due to the Coronavirus. The last time I went to that shopping center, I found out he had already left Qatar. His former co-worker told me, he left Qatar on 25th January 2021.

Rezaul works as a cleaner in the 76-storey Sulafa Tower. He came from the Laxmipur district of Bangladesh. In the year 2012, I lived on the 68th floor of this Sulafa Tower in Dubai Marina. That was where I met Rezaul. Each floor has a garbage or trash disposal room. Residents on each floor leave trash in that room. Rezaul's job is to collect the trash from each floor and clean the trash room by throwing it down the central garbage room through a tunnel that connects all the floors. Later he goes downstairs, collects from the Central Garbage Room, and loads on the garbage trucks of Balodia (City Corporation). However, Rezaul does not do this alone; there are a few others who are also Bangladeshis.

A young staff from Magura named Zahid used to work in our cafeteria. For Americans, American dishes would always be cooked. And the staff members used to cook food for them in a different style. From the dining facility's cooks to the cleaners, the waiters, the dishwashers-all people are from the Indian sub-continent. Most are Bangladeshi; some are Nepali, Sri Lankan, and Indian. A boy from Chandpur, Bangladesh named Fayez was the night shift leader, and Zahid was a waiter.

When Zahid found out that I am from Kushtia and I was going to Bangladesh on vacation, he insisted on visiting his house to meet his family. Magura district is next to Kushtia. I told him that it takes time to go to Dhaka and Kushtia for a few days' vacation, so there is barely any time left to go anywhere else.

But I promised to talk to his family on the phone. When I went to Bangladesh and talked to Zahid's father, he repeatedly asked me to visit Magura, but I could not keep his request. I said that I would try next time. He asked me how often I got my vacation and when I would come again. I replied, "Every six months, I get two weeks' leave; I go to Bangladesh on one vacation and America on the other." He said, "Son, you get so much leave, and my Zahid gets leave only once in two or three years and that too for a month!" How I can explain to the gentleman that two people's job is not the same, or that Bangladesh will have to wait a long time to cross the line drawn between the green and blue passports in the present world.

By the way, I must highlight here a real experience of my life. In 2013, I went to Saudi Arabia to perform the holy Hajj (pilgrimage). The Saudi government significantly reduced the number of Hajj pilgrims due to extensive construction work in Makkah. Although I was in the UAE, but I got a Saudi visa under the Bangladeshi quota with my friend Harun's help. I had to go from Dubai to Saudi Arabia. Upon arriving at Jeddah Airport around noon, I saw many Bangladeshis doing various jobs at the airport. Some of them helped me pick up my luggage. When I was taken to the area designated for Bangladeshi pilgrims, I came across a crowd; there were myriad people awaiting their turn. Seeing the blue US passport in my hand, the Saudi official tailgated me to the passport desk where the passport officer was about to seal my passport. However, he noticed that my visa was issued under the Bangladeshi quota. He immediately returned the papers and asked me to join the queue. Finally, after waiting for about nine hours, I was able to get on the bus at 9 pm to be ferried to Mecca after lots of hassle.

I saw many people were still waiting. In Mina and Arafat Square, I also noticed Bangladeshis living in remote areas and Americans residing in air-conditioned tents next to the metro station. Even in the holiest places of Islam, the gap between blue and green passports is visible.

Then when I talked to Mrs. Zahid on the phone, I had another incredible experience. It seemed that the lady took the phone from her father-in-law and went to her room to talk. She informed me that no one in that house liked her. Earlier, Zahid used to send money to her, but now he sends it to his father. Earlier, she had a mobile phone, which was seized. The house's people harbored the notion that she must be involved in an illicit relationship as she was living without the husband. She had two school-going children- a boy and a girl. The boy had a mobile phone, but his mother was not allowed to have one. Alas, the social system of Bangladesh! On one hand, the lady is living a lonely life without her husband, and on the other, the doubt and ignorance of the family members of the house- both are making her life impoverished. She repeatedly asked me to explain to Zahid that he didn't need to work abroad; he should come back and live with his wife and children. Whenever she got a chance to call me, she made the same request.

"Blood-red roses of thousands of minds, tears fall like the dew
How many people die of heartache?
Empty souls are crying out for a call today."

Artist: Abdul Jabbar
Lyricist: Mutafizur Rahman
Composer: Satya Saha

Chapter 3

Misconception About the Middle East

The majority of Bangladeshis think that landing the opportunity to go abroad means getting their hands on the wild goose. To them, going abroad means being able to solve all the problems of the family. That's why they sell their land and borrow a considerable amount of money to come to the Middle East to catch the wild goose. But only the one who has gone abroad knows that the reality is callous. In most cases, it is only the one-way ticket as the opportunity to get off the grinding wheel lays at distant horizons. Because after arriving at the Middle East airports, the employer's first task is to collect passports from everyone and keep those to themselves. So, no matter how much cruelty these employees face, they cannot escape. Though some people have managed to flee but they cannot return to the homeland without their passport. They even do not have the privilege of going to the police as either they will be put behind the bars due to lack of passport or sent back to their previous employer. Thus, they press forward slowly to their grave cemented on foreign land. There is no one to hear their tight-lipped yowls. Apart from the family, Bangladesh Embassy too is out of their reach. In most cases, it has become almost impossible to get help from the Bangladesh Mission.

"Exhaling, this side of the river says
All the happiness lies on the flip-side, I believe
The flip-side wails and says
That side is bursting at the seams with bliss."

- Rabindranath Tagore

Therefore, I strongly recommend that the Bangladesh government should appoint the most experienced and capable diplomats in the Middle East instead of focusing only on Europe or the United States. But the irony is that the Western countries top the charts in terms of preference than the Middle Eastern countries. The hard-earned foreign currency of the Middle East workers is smuggled back to Europe and America for creating massive infrastructure and business. There is no one to notice or address this issue. For the last eight years, I have been observing the doomed souls' silent tears and hearing their heartbreaking stories.

"Everyone is crying in the morning
Listen, listen oh father
Whisper to ear
Listen to blessing with all your heart

What would happen, Lord of the worlds
Where is peace
Let the peace prevail, give us hope,
You come closer."
— Rabindranath Tagore

There is a huge contradiction between Bangladesh and its neighboring countries in terms of migration. Anshuman Sarker's home is at Krishanagar in Nadia located on the other side of the border in Bangladesh's Kushtia district. Becoming an Indian citizen, he could travel across the borders free of cost; he didn't even have to pay for the airfare. Sharbindu Mandal from Kolkata in West Bengal said precisely the same thing. He informed me that he worked at Dammam in Saudi Arabia from 2015 to 2018 as a cook. In the same post, a boy named Raihan Chowdhury came from Noakhali, Bangladesh, at the cost of 8 lakh taka (0.8 million) (around 9300 USD). When the contract ended after three years, Sharbindu returned to the country without hesitation and later came to Qatar. However, he doesn't know what happened to Raihan, a Bangladeshi who spent an immense fortune working there. Who knows how many more years Raihan will have to stay in Saudi Arabia to earn back that considerable sum. Being an Indian passport holder, the monthly salary of Anshuman and Sharbindu is 1800 Qatari riyal (around 490 USD). Contrastingly, Nayan, Zakir,

Akter, Mallik, and many other Bangladeshi have worked in the same place and at the same designation. Despite spending lots of money to attain the work visa, their salary is about 1200 Qatar riyal (around 330 USD). And why is there a difference? Well, just because they are Bangladeshi passport holders.

It is pertinent to mention here that some Bangladeshi workers came here through a company, GSCS, which later lost the contract with the USA government. Many of them came to me grief-stricken and asked me to do something. They came to this country just a few months ago through agents to catch the wild goose. It will take them a few years to earn that money. There is no way to go back to the country empty-handed and turn a blind eye to the lenders. I told them to talk to the new company (VECTRUS). VECTRUS allowed them to work, but the old company (GSCS) didn't release a NOC (No Objection Certificate) for them to work in the new company. As a result, many of them who had spent a lot of money had to return to Bangladesh after working for only a few months. Changing 'kafala' in the Middle East means moving from one job to another, and it is a death trap. Many people get a good job but can't change the company because of this NOC problem. The famous lyricist Gauriprashanna Mojumdar once wrote, "*O river...you break one coast, build another...but those who have lost both sides, what do you have for them? I am sure the river doesn't have an answer to the question; actually, no one has!*"

As the senior officers of VECTRUS are Indians, they opened an office in India, hired all the workers directly, and brought them here free of cost. That's why at present, instead of the Bangladeshi, Nepali, Sri Lankan workers; the workers from different provinces of India, including West Bengal, Tamil Nadu, and so on, can only be seen. No Bangladeshi can be found among the workers there. Everyone had to stay at home for six months because of Corona Virus, but they got full payment. Needless to say, we have stopped them from working here because of Covid-19. No one knows the whereabouts of the Bangladeshi who came here in exchange for millions in such difficult times. The heartbreaking emptiness of unfortunate people like Hossein can be heard through the artist Abdul Jabbar's voice written for the movie "Ektuku Asha" in 1968, wherein the lyricist was Mohammed. Moniruzzaman and the composer was Satya Saha, *"Newspaper comes every day filled with much news… Lots of news of life remains concealed…"*

~~~

> *"Wrong does not leave without consequences*
> *After losing everything, my zero is not accounted for.*
> *God inks the fate*
> *The fame is for the donor*
> *A thousand bows for that donor."*
>
> Artist: *Manna Dey*
> Lyricist: *Pulak Banerjee*

~~~

Chapter 4

The Horrible Incident at Holy Artisan

It was during the month of Ramadan when I came to UAE for the second time on June 30, 2016, at 9:45 pm. I stayed in Hotel Ibis in Abu Dhabi for some time as the designated villa was under construction. As it was the month of Ramadan, so the workload was a little less. Hence, I was spending my time idly; watching television and taking rest. On July 01, I turned on the television and saw an extremely unpleasant massacre incident that took place in a restaurant in the Gulshan diplomatic area of Dhaka, Bangladesh. CNN, BBC, Al Jazeera, all the news channels were stormed with the news of the same incident. Sadly, there was no Bangladeshi TV channel in the hotel, so I tried to find out the real facts by collecting news from those channels. After listening to the news all night, still, no details were known. I called a friend of mine, Harun, who lives in that area in Dhaka, and tried to find out the real story.

Surprisingly, despite living in the same country, they do not know even as much we know sitting abroad. When I was a kid, my father's friend joked saying that you must listen to foreign news channels such as the BBC and Voice of America to know about the country's information. During my childhood days, there was only one government TV channel (BTV) in Bangladesh. However, in 2016, when there was a multitude of private TV channels, I did not know that the situation was still the same. I was horrified by the news I received the next day, on July 02. A restaurant called Holy Artisan in Gulshan had witnessed one of the most dreadful incidents in the history of independent Bangladesh. The severity of the incident could not be imagined at first. When the Bangladesh Army's commando unit completed the rescue operation under Operation Thunderbolt about 12 hours later, the world was astonished to see the turbulent environment prevailing in peace-loving moderate Muslim Bangladesh. Nine Italians, seven Japanese, one American, one Indian, and six Bangladeshis were brutally slaughtered in the name of religion by seven or eight young fanatics. I have heard the immortal saying of religion, "Islam is the religion of peace." In Bangladesh, where 90% of the population is Muslim, it seems that neither the government nor the general public would have imagined that anyone could commit such a heinous crime. Alas! Bigotry does not allow the man to be human anymore. Look at the newspaper of that day. You can see some hints regarding the identity of the killers' mental perversion and the inhumanity, horror, violence, and cruelty of the incident.

"The Islamists, who carried out Bangladesh's terror worst attack at a cafe here, had slaughtered all the 20 hostages within 20 minutes of the brazen assault, a top police official said today." (The Economic Times: July 04, 2016)

"The gunmen then separated the Muslims from the non-Muslims. The Muslims were given food and water, while the non-Muslims were not." (CNN: July 05, 2016)

"An Indian woman who had been badly injured was moaning in agony, but a perpetrator took a sword to her and killed her without mercy." (Daily Star: July 07, 2016)

Foreigners are considered guests in the country. I have heard somewhere that there is a sacred instruction of religion to treat guests graciously. Allah has declared in the Holy Qur'an to be kind to everyone.

The Almighty Allah says in Surah An-Nisa, verse 36:

وَاعْبُدُوا اللَّهَ وَلَا تُشْرِكُوا بِهِ شَيْئًا ۖ وَبِالْوَالِدَيْنِ إِحْسَانًا وَبِذِي الْقُرْبَىٰ وَالْيَتَامَىٰ وَالْمَسَاكِينِ وَالْجَارِ ذِي الْقُرْبَىٰ وَالْجَارِ الْجُنُبِ وَالصَّاحِبِ بِالْجَنبِ وَابْنِ السَّبِيلِ وَمَا مَلَكَتْ أَيْمَانُكُمْ ۗ إِنَّ اللَّهَ لَا يُحِبُّ مَن كَانَ مُخْتَالًا فَخُورًا

"Worship Allah alone and associate none with Him. And be kind to parents, relatives, orphans, the poor, near and distant neighbors, close friends, ˹needy˺ travelers, and those ˹bonds people˺ in your possession. Surely Allah does not like whoever is arrogant, boastful." (4:36)

Never mind the good behavior; it took me a few more days to find out how and where the mentality of slaughtering for the sake of religion came from. It is essential for the development of humanity that manners be beautiful. The real identity of the man is revealed through his behavior. Whether a person is good or bad can be judged by his manners. The scars of the 9/11 incident had not yet healed and now this incident on the soil of my birthland boggled my mind again.

In 1971, trampling the theory of Muslim brotherhood, the Pakistanis were the murderers, and we were the victims. But today, we are murderers, and foreign guests are our victims. Humanity means love, affection, tenderness for other human beings. People learn about humanity from childhood from family, school, society, and the state. Unfortunately, humanity is in question today as it has become the interest of most individuals to capitalize on religion and politics. Greed, power, envy, and inhuman morals are destroying humanity. The man himself is again destroying the transformation from man to humankind.

> *"Hearing 'I am Hindu' and 'I am Muslim' constantly made my ears tingle. But I don't hear people say, 'I am human'. Those who are not human cannot make any difference in the world, whether they are Hindus or Muslims."*
>
> *-Rabindranath Tagore*

Chapter 5

Bangladesh: Then and Now

I stayed in the hotel for the rest of Ramadan. The first time, I stayed in the UAE for four years from 2012 to 2016. The United Arab Emirates is known as UAE for the whole world. However, the name 'Dubai' is better known to most people in Bangladesh. Probably, the introduction of Dubai gained more popularity from the dialog *"teha den Dubai jabo (give me money I want to go to Dubai)"* of a popular Bangladeshi drama starring Amjad Hossain and Farid Ali.

Although it was born just 14 days before the independence of Bangladesh, the UAE's state structure, communication system, law, and order, the social image can be compared to any other developing country globally. It is constitutionally an Islamic republic; just as Muslims live here with their culture and civilization, so do the Westerners with their behavior and culture. Some men could be walking around wearing Arabic Dishdashah or thawb/thobe on the same street or in a shopping center, just as others walking around wearing T-shirts and shorts. There is no exception in women either; some walk around wearing hijab or niqab (a head covering worn by some Muslim women), while others wear jeans, T-shirts, or any western dress without any hesitation or fear. No one in this country has a headache regarding this social system. I have not seen any tendency to force one's culture on another. Citizens of other countries have full freedom in this regard. It does not affect one's caste or religion, nor does it hurt one's religious feelings. No one protests in the streets in the name of defending Islam because Islam is not threatened or the faith is not endangered at all. *"It was said that religion would save people. From the day people started defending religion, trouble started."*

~~~

That is why the Baul emperor Lalon has said:
"Caste is gone, Caste has vanished
What a weird cry all over
None is ready to do the right thing
Everyone seems to be merely stuck in the rut."

-Lalon Shah

~~~

If the same thing had happened in Bangladesh, then the sentimental Bangladeshi brothers would have flown a river of blood in the streets. Let alone wearing T-shirts, I have heard that when women go out without hijab, they become an eyesore for many. A few days ago, through social media, I saw a comparison of a picture of Dhaka University from the '70s with another photo from 2019. The difference between the then progressive Dhaka University image and today's religious and sentimental university is sky-high.

১৯৭১ বনাম ২০১৯ এর বাংলাদেশ।

Bangladesh 1971 vs. 2019

Needless to say, when Saudi Arabia, the United Arab Emirates, Bahrain, and other Arab countries in the Middle East are moving towards some reforms, Bangladesh is losing its secularism and becoming a super-Islamic state today. The far-sightedness of predicting the result seems beyond the reach of Bangladeshi political leaders. Women have been allowed to drive in the UAE since the inception, women in Saudi Arabia; the holiest Islamic site, have been allowed to drive since June 24, 2018. Precisely nine months later, a report published in the Saudi Gazette in March 2019 quoted Maj. Gen. Mohammed Al-Bassami, a top Saudi Traffic official, said that at least 70,000 women had been issued driving licenses.

70,000 women obtain Saudi driving licenses

*BURAIDAH — As many as 70,000 women have been issued driving licenses since June 24, 2018, when authorities lifted the ban on women driving in Saudi Arabia, according to Director. General of Traffic Maj. Gen. Mohammed Al-Bassami (**Saudi Gazette report:** March 19, 2019)*

"The kingdom's ambitious de facto ruler, Crown Prince Mohammed bin Salman, has introduced multiple economic and social innovations in a kingdom where uncompromising religious police once severely curtailed public life. Under the reform drive, women are allowed to take the wheel of cars after a decades-old driving ban was scrapped and permitted to go to stadiums to watch sports and concerts.

Cinemas were reopened after many years of closures, noisy parties are permitted, and authorities turn a blind eye as shops remain open during prayer times -- a grave offense in the past. The metamorphosis has been widely welcomed in a country with a large youth population and endorsed by clerics perceived to be pro-government. But some conservative Saudis beg to differ, even if they do so quietly for fear of punishment.

Loud musical parties, mixing of the sexes and easing restrictions on the female dress code -- these were all unthinkable just a few years ago and are not permissible in the home of the two holy mosques," said Ibrahim, a 55-year old Arabic teacher."

- Arabian Business, Sat February 1, 2020

My mother and sisters have never worn hijab over their heads but perform the salah (prayer) five times a day and fast during Ramadan. And now, in 90% of Islamic religious Bangladesh, women are seen walking around the shopping malls wearing the hijab during the Maghrib (evening salah). They roam freely in shopping malls and near the university, in Sohrawardi Udyan, Ramna Park, in front of Eden College, and many more places. They do not even have time to perform the short stretched Maghrib salah (prayer). Seeing their actions, it seems that they have chosen the hijab as a fashion instead of a religious instruction. Who has more religious feelings among them can be a matter of debate. The Indian subcontinent has been divided into two halves because of religion, but the fractionalized Pakistan could not be held united in the name of religion. In my early years, the house of the famous playwright 'Kalyan Mitra' was next to ours. Saraswati (Goddess of knowledge, music, art, and wisdom) Puja (festival) was performed every year in the field in front of his house. Our brothers and sisters were so happy to go to that field, and we would bring the petals of the flowers from Swarasati Puja and put them inside books. I don't know if this scenario is still there in Bangladesh. But now, let alone worship, it has become haram (prohibited) to call *'pani'* (water) as *'jal'*. I would like to know whether in the present textbook *'Jalprapat'* (falls) i.e. Niagara Falls,.is written as *'Paniprapat'* or *'Pani-path'* war is called as *'Jal-path'* war in India. I don't even know when the word "Khoda-Hafez" (goodbye) I had learned as a child became "Allah-Hafez". Now the picture of difference among us is visible.

"We used to spend beautiful days
We used to have a splendid time
The village youth, Hindu and Muslim
We used to sing Baul and Murshidi songs together.

Jatra songs were sung in Hindu homes
They invited, and we abided,
Jari songs, Baul songs
Surged a spring of joy,
We used to run towards the boat singing Shari songs.

When the rain kissed the ground
Gazi's song echoed,
We sang in styles
We became happy.
Who would be the member,
Or be the government?
Did we care about such enigmas?
Did we care about getting the news?
What beautiful days! We used to spend.

Today, we think cheerlessly
We would not get those merry days back
There was a desire to be happy,
Day after day
Time becomes more rigid."

—Baul Shah Abdul Karim

Chapter 6

UAE:
The Country in Detail

The United Arab Emirates, the southeastern countryside of the Arabian Peninsula, covers an area of 83,600 square kilometers (32,278 square miles). The capital and largest city of the federation, Abu Dhabi, is located in the emirate of the same name. Abu Dhabi covers 67,340 square kilometers (26,000 square miles), or 86.7% of its total area. Dubai covers 3,885 square kilometers (1500 square miles), equivalent to 5% of its total area. The area of Sharjah is 2590 square kilometers (1000 square miles). The northern emirates, including Fujairah, Ajman, Ras al-Khaimah, and Umm al-Quwain, have a total area of 3,881 square kilometers (1,998 square miles). According to the World Bank, the population of the UAE in 2018 was 9.53 million. 35.6% (3.3 million) of the total population lives in Dubai, 34.7% (3.2 million) in Abu Dhabi, 16.2% (1.5 million) in Sharjah and 5.8% (540,000) in Ajman, 4.1% (390,000) in Ras-al-Khaimah, 2.7% (250,000) in Fujairah, and 0.9% (80,000) in Umm-al-Quwain. The expatriate population is 88.52%, and the remaining 11.48% are Emirati.

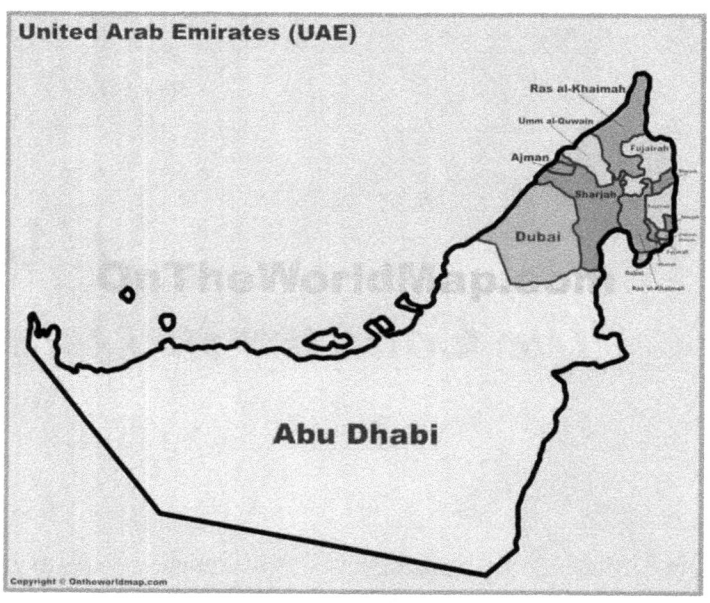

The United Arab Emirates coast stretches for about 650 kilometers (404 miles) along the southern coast of the Persian Gulf. The six states of the emirate are located along the Persian Gulf, and Fujairah on the east coast, the seventh state is on the Gulf of Oman. Saudi Arabia borders the region to the southwest, Oman to the east and northeast, the Persian Gulf to the southeast, and the Gulf of Oman to the northwest. The coast area formed a federation of 6 states on December 2, 1971, known as the UAE on the world map. Of the current seven states in the UAE, the first six states Abu Dhabi, Dubai, Sharjah, Ajman, Umm-al-Quwain, and Fujairah, joined the new state. About two months later, on February 10, 1972,

Ras-al-Khaimah joined the Federation of the UAE. Initially, Bahrain and Qatar were supposed to enter the new state, but they declared themselves separate independent states due to differences among themselves. Sheikh Zayed bin Sultan Al Nahyan is the founding father of the ethnically diverse UAE. The UAE is ethnically diverse. The total expatriate population is about 8.45 million.

The expatriate population of UAE in 2018:

Nationality	Population
India	2.62 million
Pakistan	1.21 million
Bangladesh	0.71 million
Philippine	0.53 million
Iran	0.45 million
Egypt	0.40 million
Nepal	0.30 million
Sri Lanka	0.30 million
China	0.20 million
Other countries	1.71 million

Source: statistica.com

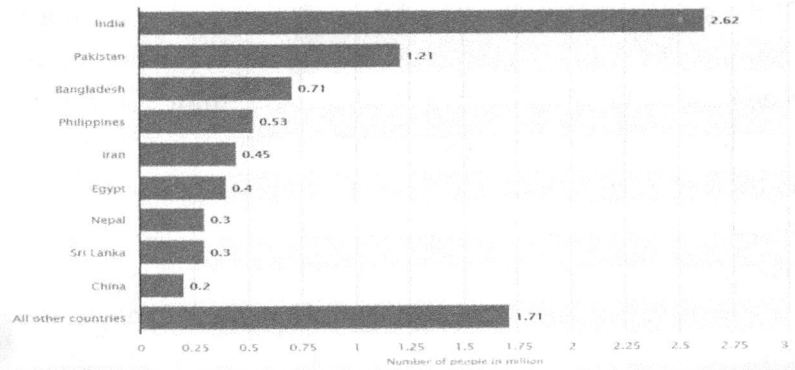

Source: statistica.com

The United Arab Emirates is constitutionally a federal monarchy, and the political system is called the Sheikhdoms. Abu Dhabi, Ajman, Fujairah, Sharjah, Dubai, Ras al-Khaimah, and Umm al-Quwain are governed by a Federal Supreme Council consisting of ruling Sheiks. The seven hereditary monarchy-type tribes rule the seven kingdoms. Sheikh uses the title instead of Amir to refer to the individual emirates' rulers (states). The title is used because of the Sheikhdom-style governing system in keeping with the tribal culture of Arabia. Sheikh means prominent leader or tribal chief of a tribe. All responsibilities assigned to the government are reserved for a separate emirate. The percentage of revenue from each emirate is allocated to the UAE's central budget.

The Federal Supreme Council elects the President and Prime Minister. Usually, there is a Sheikh President from Abu Dhabi and a Sheikh Prime Minister from Dubai. All other prime ministers serve as vice-presidents. Sheikh Zayed bin Sultan Al Nahyan is the United Arab Emirates' founding father and widely acclaimed for uniting the seven emirates into one country. Until his death on November 2, 2004, he was the first President of the United Arab Emirates since its inception.

Of the seven UAE states, Abu Dhabi, Dubai, and Sharjah are economically self-sufficient, but the other four are not. It has been said that when Dubai opened up everything for foreign investment, local religious leaders opposed it. Their idea was that if foreigners enter their country, the country will become impure. They might do anti-social activities. Therefore, the visionary ruler of Dubai, Sheikh Mohammed bin Rashid Al Maktoum summoned all religious leaders to the palace and warned, "It is my job to rule the state, and it is your job to spread the message of religious peace. All those who disobey me in the future will be severely punished."

In most cases, severe punishment means beheading with the sword. Since then, no one has ever stopped working for the state. Every Friday, the Imams stand on the minbars during the 'Jummah khutbah' (a Muslim sermon delivered on a Friday) and wish for the King's good health and longevity. It is worth mentioning here that the speeches are also written from the Central Surah Council, and the Imam's job is to recite only that printed message and nothing more should be said.

The UAE has a diverse society. While Abu Dhabi's economy is dependent on fuel oil, Dubai's economy is heavily reliant on international trade and tourism. That is why Dubai is more open to visitors and the hub of West and Asian business. It is a sizeable global transport hub for passengers and cargo. In the early twentieth century, the center of regional and international trade, Dubai's economy depended on income from international trade, tourism, aviation, real estate, and financial services.

Emirates Airlines has a huge role to play in the economic development of Dubai. In the early 70s, Gulf Airlines was running a flat business. Therefore, in the middle of this decade, Gulf Airlines suddenly decided to cancel its services in Dubai. The airline decided to operate flights only to Abu Dhabi. Al Maktoum, the visionary ruler of Dubai, was initially worried but later decided that Dubai would launch its own airline and allocate 10 million US dollars. Maurice Flanagan, who previously worked for British Airways, Gulf Air, and BOAC and supervised Donata, was appointed chief executive of the new airline. Sheikh Ahmed bin Sayed Al Maktoum, the ruler's 26-year-old nephew, joined the airport as chairman. The situation was not conducive to purchasing new aircraft, as half of the money allocated for ancillary work was spent. At that time, Pakistan International Airlines (PIA) provided technical and administrative support to the new carrier and leased a new Boeing 737-300 and an Airbus A300 B4-200 to establish Emirates. In addition, the Royal Family's Dubai Royal Air Wing provided the airline with two older Boeings 727-200. On October 25, 1985, the airline's first flight (the EK-600) was from Dubai, UAE, to Karachi, Pakistan.

In its first year of success, Emirates Airlines carried 260,000 passengers and 10,000 tons of cargo. Gulf Air, meanwhile, saw a 56% drop in profits in its first year in the UAE and more losses in the following year. Emirates Airlines was one of the fastest-growing airlines in the world in the early nineties. In the very early 1990s, Emirates' revenue was around $100 million each year and had increased to a number close to $500 million by 1993. In the same year, the airline carried 1.6 million passengers and 68,000 tons of cargo. Emirates Airlines is the largest airline in the Middle East. It currently operates more than 3,600 flights per week to more than 150 cities in 60 countries on six continents with a fleet of 300 aircraft. (Source: Emirates Airlines)

Dubai's economy began to explode soon after the launch of Emirates Airlines. It is essential to mention here that the Biman Bangladesh Airlines was flown a decade before Emirates Airlines' birth. It was established on February 4, 1972, as the National Airline of Bangladesh under the Bangladesh Aviation Ordinance (Presidential Order No. 126). As of January 2020, the airline operated flights to 16 international and six domestic destinations. At present, there are a total of 18 airlines in the fleet, both large and small.

I once had the experience of traveling by Biman Bangladesh Airlines in the '90s. It was the month of December when I was going to Bangladesh along with my little son, who was one and a half years old. Initially, we were scheduled to fly on Thai Airways during the winter break. Thai planes used to land in Seattle, Washington at that time. However, due to heavy snowfall, the flight was delayed. As a result, the connecting flight from Bangkok to Dhaka was missed. Thai Airways then arranged Bangladesh Biman for the rest of the route.

While onboard Thai Airways from Seattle to Bangkok, I didn't have to worry about my son anymore. For a while, the flight attendants (air hostesses) came and asked if my son would need milk, diapers, etc., and they were very prompt in delivering those things. They gave my son few toys to play with and played with him whenever they got free time. Of course, they deserve admiration for customer service. But the situation was completely different on the Bangladesh Biman flight from Bangkok to Dhaka. My son was sleeping at the time regular meals were served. So, I told the attendants that I would let them know when my son would wake up later. When the time came, I took my son to the flight attendants' designated place and saw that they were busy chatting. I asked for the milk, and they told me that I should wash the feeder (milk bottle) from the toilet and give it to them, and then they would provide milk. I was a little shocked because, on the previous flight, the flight attendants cleaned the feeder with hot water every time and disinfected it. Contrarily on Biman, instead of giving the service, they were gossiping and asked me to wash the feeder from the toilet! That was the first and definitely last time in 40 years I traveled by Biman Bangladesh Airlines.

Many of us may have the misconception that Emirates Airlines is built on oil money. But I have already mentioned that there is no oil in Dubai, Abu Dhabi has the fortune, and its' national airline is 'Etihad Airways'. Dubai does not run on Abu Dhabi's oil money in the federal system. Emirates Airlines has successfully converted world-class transport due to their customer service, the right decision, visionary leader, and patriotism. Every day it operates flights to New York, Washington, Boston, Chicago, Dallas, Houston, Los Angeles, San Francisco, and Seattle in the United States with full capacity.

On the other hand, Biman's one and only Dhaka to New York flight have been suspended since July 2000 due to loss. How can I hide my grief? It's a massive, colossal failure. There should not be any excuse for it. The government should investigate the matter and find the truth.

Chapter 7

Moving to Villas and Meeting Hossein

The villa that was arranged for me in Khalifa City, a suburb of Abu Dhabi, was not ready yet. During the month of Ramadan, most of the places here work a half-day. I was looking for the progress of the work almost every day. I realized that the timeline to complete the project certainly would not be met before Eid. Usually, I don't have to go anywhere in Ramadan either. So, there was no significant work other than working a half-day and returning to the hotel room to watch television. I did not have any car of my own then. It was not possible to rent a car in this country without a national identity card, even though I had a valid UAE driving license. I got a driving license that was valid for ten years. However, last time, before leaving the country, I submitted my identity card according to the country's rules. It usually takes two to four weeks to get a new ID card, but everything is oddly slow-paced during the month of Ramadan, so there was no exact schedule of when the card would arrive.

I spent the Eid day in the hotel room casually on Wednesday, July 6, 2016. My former friends invited me to come to Sharjah and Dubai to celebrate Eid with them. The last time I was in Dubai for about four years (from the beginning of 2012 to the end of 2015), but I was in Abu Dhabi for the second time. The distance between Dubai and Abu Dhabi is a little more than 150 km. As I had no car, I could not meet the invitation of my friends. I spent the Eid day lying down and watching TV. In the afternoon, I bought a burger from the hotel lobby cafe and finished my Eid meal.

Meanwhile, on July 8, I saw on TV news that a man named Micah Xavier Johnson had shot dead five police officers and wounded nine others in Dallas, Texas. I was worried about my family because my family lives near that city. I confirmed their wellbeing on the phone and inquired about the horror of the situation.

The New York Times reported on July 8, 2016

> *"The heavily armed sniper who gunned down police officers in downtown Dallas, leaving five of them dead, specifically set out to kill as many white officers as he could, officials said Friday. He was a military veteran who had served in Afghanistan, and he kept an arsenal in his home that included bomb-making materials.*
>
> *The gunman turned a demonstration against fatal police shootings this week of black men in Minnesota and Louisiana from a peaceful march focused on violence*

committed by officers into a scene of chaos and bloodshed aimed against them."

Source: https://www.nytimes.com/2016/07/09/us/dallas-police-shooting.html?auth=login-google1tap&login=google1tap

After Eid, my villa was ready on Monday, July 11. At noon, my colleague Bill Facio came to give me a ride on his Ford pick-up. After a final check out from the Ibis Hotel, I arrived at the new villa with my friend Bill. The authorities (my employer) had already allocated money to buy the furniture. My co-worker Bill and I had already purchased some furniture from the Home Box Furniture Store on Friday, July 8. They were supposed to deliver the things after the villa was ready when I give them a call. All the furniture was set with delivery on that day after I called. I bought other necessary items as well from the local IKEA. After moving there, I realized that there was much faulty artistry that seemed completed in a hurry. Despite repeated requests, the manager in charge of the villa continued to procrastinate. The villa owner was an Emirati, but the person in charge of the management was an Egyptian. Since I had signed the contract and moved into the villa, the gentleman believed it shouldn't be given much importance at the moment. Once the contract has been signed, ordinary people are not left with many options after moving into a home.

But in my case, it was a little different. The gentleman in charge of management, Tariq, told my boss that he did not want to deal with the Americans and was arrogant about the United States. At the time, a Tunisian Muslim, Mohamed Lahouaiej-Bouhlel, deliberately drove a 19-ton cargo truck over a crowd during the Bastille Day celebration in Nice, France, Thursday, July 14, killing 86 people and injuring 458 others. The very next day, on July 15, a section of the Turkish military tried to overthrow the government and President Recep Tayyip Erdoğan in the bloodiest coup in its political history. The Turkish army landed in Ankara and Istanbul with tanks. The country faced its fourth devastating military coup in its 95-year political history. Thousands of ordinary citizens marched the streets for protest. With the help of loyal soldiers and police forces, the coup attempt was defeated. In less than half a month since the beginning of July, the world had been witnessing one incident after another, starting with the Holy Artisan of Bangladesh, then in Dallas, USA, in Nice, France, and most recently in Turkey. After the choicest remarks of Mr. Tariq, who was in charge of the villa, my superiors became concerned about the security. After the intervention of my superiors, my employer rented another villa and paid one year's rent in advance. My boss instructed me to move to the new villa very quickly.

So I had to move again in a week. That time, moving to another house was a little more troublesome. There was no furniture when I came from the hotel, but later, I had to take some furniture and other accessories with me. So professional movers had to be hired to move the things, and my authorities arranged it. On July 20, when I was going to enter the second villa for the first time, I saw a young dark-brown man watering a date tree in the house next door. It was the middle of the day and he was watering under the scorching midday sun. He looked like a Bangladeshi. Although I have been living in the United States for almost 35 years after leaving Bangladesh, but whenever I see a local, I yearn to talk to the person; I wish to speak in Bengali. It is tough to forget the roots.

So, I stopped the car, lowered the window, and asked the lad what country was he from. He replied with a smile on his face, "Bangladesh." Then I asked him in Bengali, "What is your name, and which district are you from?" Seeing me speaking in Bengali, he flashed his 100-watt beam. Joyfully he came near me and replied that he was from Laxmipur and his name was Hossein. He had been working there for five years. Then Hossein asked me in return, "Are you Bangladeshi (in the Bengali language)?" I also racked up and replied, "That's why I am speaking Bengali." I told him that I would move into the villa next door and meet him later. Since then, I have known Hossein. For the next three months, he was my acquaintance with whom I spoke in Bengali. He has shared many stories of his happiness and sorrow with me. I have heard many more fragmentary stories before but haven't had the opportunity or the misfortune to get to know them so closely.

Hossein comes from Uttar Char Banshi village of Raipur Thana in the Laxmipur district of southeastern Bangladesh. He was born in 1980. He is a child from an impoverished ordinary family of rural Bengal. His father, Mr. Ali Ahmad, worked as a housekeeper. With a son and a daughter in their early years, his first wife died due to illness, and then he married Hossein's mother. Hossein's mother gave birth to two daughters and seven sons. Hossein is the third among the nine. He has a mother, wife, one son, one daughter, one brother, brother's wife, and their two daughters back in his home. Hossein has to bear all the expenses of such a big family. All the sisters are married; all the other brothers are separated except one.

After marrying in 2001 and becoming a father of a daughter, he moved to Abu Dhabi on November 23, 2011. The boy was born later after he came to Abu Dhabi. Hossein used to work as a carpenter in Bangladesh. He got his visa for the UAE by giving one lakh seventy thousand (170,000) (around 1,970 USD) taka to a broker. He borrowed the money from one of his neighbors in exchange for interest. For this, he had to pay more than two lakh taka (around 2,317 USD) later. It took about 3-4 years to repay this money. The girl is in sixth grade (at the time this book is being written), and the boy is 2016-born.

Eight months after Hossein arrived in Abu Dhabi, his father died at the age of eighty. At that time, his younger brother was working in the police force. He quit because of the hardships of the job. Hossein saved some money by working hard, borrowed the rest from his friends, and sent his younger brother to Oman at the cost of three and a half lakh taka (Tk. 3 50,000) (around 4,055 USD). But his brother did not like the hard-working life in Oman, too, so he returned home after a few months and started working as a painter. Things that are not achieved through hard work have no value. Hossein now bears the expenses of this brother and his family.

I later found out that Bangladeshi boys work in almost all the houses and villas on that street and even Bangladeshi girls also work in a few places. A Bengali girl named Taslima works in Hossein's owner's house. Among the working people are some Nepalese and some Filipinos. Through Hossein, I met many Bangladeshi young men working on that road. Some of them are from Noakhali, some from Sylhet, some from Chittagong, and one of them from Gopalganj. Mr. Taibur Rahman from Gopalganj used to work in BDR (Border guard), Bangladesh before coming to Abu Dhabi.

I regularly go for a walk in the afternoon; I try to walk five to ten km (3.1 miles to 6.2 miles) daily. I prefer going out for a walk a little earlier in the evening, avoiding going out in the afternoon in extreme heat (50° C or 122° F). I often see Hossein watering the trees wearing pants and T-shirts. Whenever Hossein sees me, no matter what condition he is in, he would leave his work, run to me, greet me with a big smile, and ask, "Sir, would you like to eat some dates?" Before I could say anything, Hossein would climb a small ladder attached to the little date tree. From there, he would collect half-ripe dates for me, wash them from the faucet outside, and forcefully put them in my hand. It is worth mentioning here that every house has a tap water connection outside the boundary wall for general use. Anyone can use this water if they wish. It is open to all travelers. Even though I have stopped Hossein a thousand times, he would still not listen and would say with a smile, "Sir eat, it is good for health. Keep walking and munching."

Dates plucked from someone else's yard was a matter of dilemma for me; I would lose the language to disappoint his smiling face. I used to say to him, "Hossein, if you give me dates, your employer will be angry with you." Hossein would reply with a smile, "No problem, my boss says you can give dates to everyone; giving dates is a good deed." So no more objections would stand. I used to practice my daily evening walk with the dates in my hand, and at the same time, I would gently run the dates, collected from the fresh tree given by Hossein, into my mouth. When I came back, I used to see Hossein talking to some friends, some of them talking with their family back in the country via Facebook, and some watching dramas on YouTube. After a hard day's work, they enjoy the evening as they wish. Several boys have sprinklers in their owner's house. So, they would leave the sprinkler open and come back to talking, and from time to time, they would get up, turn off one sprinkler and turn on another. However, I didn't see any sprinklers in Hossein's house, so Hossein had to hold a water pipe and water different trees.

The house that Hossein works in is built on more than an acre of land. There are many date palms inside and outside. There are other trees, high boundary walls all around with a giant building in the middle (it can be called a mansion). The vast house has many rooms, but there is no room for Hossein to stay. He is accommodated in a small hut-like room built along the boundary wall after crossing the main gate of the boundary wall and going a hundred yards to the right, in the alley to the back of the house. After walking hundreds of yards along that alley, a small room is built for male staff, with a bathroom. Hossein lives there. A door to enter the house is on the side of the alley. There is no way to enter Hossein's hut through the building's central part or no windows on that side. To get to the central part of the building, Hossein always has to walk through that alley and enter through the main gate. Not only Hossein, but all the houses in the area have the same accommodation for the housemaids.

There are indoor accommodations for female employees only. Arrangements have been made for the two of them to stay in this small room, but Hossein's luck is slightly on his side. His roommate went on vacation to his motherland to get married. When he returned after the vacation, he was no longer employed in the house and was sent to work for the master's eldest son's elder wife. So, Hossein is currently living alone. His roommate's name was Saddam, and he worked as a cook in that house. After placing two beds for sleeping in the room, there is not much space left there. The male employee is called '*Khaddam*' in Arabic. The female employee is called '*Khaddama*'. Although most male employees here are Bangladeshis, but Filipinos and Nepalese predominate among female employees.

Hossein's master's name is Mr. Rashed, who works in a city council under Abu Dhabi called Baldia in Arabic. Mr. Rashed has three wives; this is his second wife's house. The master's first wife lives with their son in Al Ain, another state in the UAE. Master himself lives in another place in Abu Dhabi with his third wife and her three sons. Hossein works at his second wife's house. The mistress lives in this house with her two sons and five daughters. The eldest daughter is married, and all the other boys and girls go to school. But the master takes care of all the three houses. The master comes every one or two weeks, providing the necessary things. In Hossein's words, "Father bought groceries." Hossein calls the head of the house 'father' and the mistress 'mother'.

On that day, Hossein's duty increased a little because he had to take the goods from the master's car and wash his vehicle. Then there is the extra cooking for father. Hossein does all the chores, from taking care of the yard outside the house to cooking for the home. Although there is another female housemaid (Taslima) in the house, her only responsibility is to clean the rooms, wash and iron the clothes. The mistress and eldest daughter do not come out in front of Hossein, or even if they do, they wear a black Arabian burqa. They order over the phone or from upstairs if any work is needed to be done.

Hossein is a very loyal employee. During the Eid vacations, the house's lady and children go to her relative's house to celebrate

Eid for a few days. Once, during the Eid days, another close relative came to the house and left some jewelry in a box for the mistress. Even though Taslima was at home, the housewife called Hossein and ordered him to take custody of the jewelry and keep it in his hut. Needless to say, this incident proves that the mistress trusts Hossein more than Taslima.

A few years ago (2011), Hossein was given a job just to work in the garden. Chef Saddam was there to cook, he was the roommate in Hossein's small hut, and he was also a Bangladeshi, a resident of Narsingdi district. Hossein started working at a monthly salary of 900 dirhams (20,350 BDT) (around 240 USD). Hossein had to work all day in the hot sun outside. Hossein used to take care of the plants, keep the yard clean, water the trees, clean all the cars in the house, go to the market to buy small goods, or fulfill all the outdoor orders. The cook was paid 1600 dirhams (36,200 BDT) (around 420 USD) per month. Of course, a chef's skills and requirements are more excellent than those of a gardener or housemaid. However, under the 50° C or 122° F scorching heat of the desert, it is right to say that the work outside is no less complicated. It is challenging for those who have never felt the Middle East desert's heat to understand its painful reality. My idea is that Arabic clothes are made according to the weather to protect them from direct sunlight. Men's white thobe (<u>Arabic</u>: ثَوْبٌ) is usually long-sleeved and ankle-length, and women typically wear a black abaya (Arabic: عَبايَة) on top of any garments. These are quite the same dress.

Although Hossein was an uneducated person, but he understood the inequality. Everyone in the world, big or small, dreams of improving the living standards of themselves and their families. And everyone tries their best in the hope of fulfilling this dream. However, some become successful, and some are not but dreams never cease. A journey begins with a vision, and it is possible to accomplish the objective through hard work and perseverance. The eleventh President of India (2002-2007) - Dr. A.P.J. Abdul Kalam has said:

> *"Dreams aren't what you see when you sleep; it's something that doesn't let you sleep."*

And like ten other people, Hossein dreamed of a better future for himself and his family. That's why Hossein slowly learned to cook from his partner Saddam. He expected that if he knows cooking, he would be able to work somewhere else at a higher salary and would not have to burn in 115°/122° F or 46°/50° C temperature outside. But there is a saying, "*Man proposes, God, deposes.*" Although Hossein had become a chef, but it did not change his fate.

Shortly after Hossein took the job, his colleague went on leave to get married. Hossein's landlord became very anxious and started searching for a chef. I have heard from Hossein that the house lady doesn't even bother to cook, so it was tough for their family to eat. The master became bewildered. A chef had to be hired at any cost. The master himself started looking for a chef and told Hossein to find someone who knew how to cook. Hossein told his master with high hopes that he had learned to cook from his friend and that he too could cook for them. Upon hearing this, the master seemed to get the moon in his hand and became very happy. Hossein was immediately appointed as a cook in addition to gardening. Hossein became delighted and continued his work, and again started cooking as an additional responsibility. And he kept dreaming that this time, he would build a house in his village with the extra 1600 dirham (36,200 BDT) (around 420 USD). The mother will see the face of happiness in her last years, and at the same time, the wife and children will live well. However, days have turned into months and months into years but Hossein's salary has never increased from 900 to even 1000, let alone 2500. But as an additional responsibility, Hossein now has to do the cooking work properly. Hossein's dream of a permanent house still remains a dream. That dream can no longer become a reality; it is destroyed in the bud.

"Have you ever come eyeball-to-eyeball with the defeat of life
In the sanctuary of sorrow and the ceaseless cries, slowly his decay
I have seen so many dreams nipping in the buds
And so many sad notes playing in the dry foliage
While unmitigated hopes remain wailing in the air and sky
A boatload of news come up every day that blacken the pages of paper,
A lot of the news on the life page remains invisible
No one knows the longings of life, what it wants again and again
Why do loved ones move away due to selfish and unselfish interests?
On the surface of the earth, they live side by side,
but no one is for each other."

Artist: Abdul Jabbar
Lyricist: Mohammed Moniruzzaman
Composer: Satya Saha

Chapter 8

The Exploitation of Migrant Workers

Saddam, the chef, came back from his country a few months after his marriage, but he was no longer employed. Because there was Hossein in this house, he handled all the work inside and outside alone, so there was no need for an extra cost. Instead, Saddam was sent to Al-Ain as a cook to home of the owner's most senior wife. In the world, such Hosseins remain the same; their fate does not change. All exploiters have the same face throughout all times, all places. Hossein saved his owner's monthly 1600 dirhams (around 420 USD), but he did not get any benefit. As an additional responsibility, he now has to handle all the work outside and inside alone. Where humanity is zero, the message of religion is meaningless. It has been written that there is no difference between people. In the colonial era, masters forced servants and slaves to work for free. A servant is a person who has been enslaved. That era ended long ago in the civilized world. However, in some parts of the world, slavery is still practiced in the present age by classifying people as property under civilization's guise. The cries of these people do not enter the ears of a majority of civilized people. These damned souls shed tears for this exploited class with their inflammatory speeches in the field, they are seen sniffing, calling them 'Middle Eastern Kamlas' during the actual work. Where knowledge is limited, the reason is numb, liberation is impossible.

The 'Middle Eastern Kamla' of Bangladesh is again neglected as "Miskin" in the Middle East. A report by the United Nations International Labor Organization (ILO) estimates that about one in five of the world's migrant domestic workers lives in the Middle East. There are a total of 3.16 million domestic workers, of whom 1.6 million are women. A 2014 study conducted by Human Rights Watch found that the employers' abuse was inhumane and traumatic. There is no one to hear their heartache and cries, even the water of the Arabian Sea is flowing silently as Bhupen Babu's 'Ganga' (*"Even after hearing the cries of countless people who live in the vast stretches on your both banks, O Ganga, why do you flow?"* -Dr. Bhupen Hajarika).

Fadi al-Qadi, an Amman-based Middle East and North African human rights, civil society, and media commentator published a report in The New Arab on December 5, 2017.

> **"Gulf migrant workers are being abused in complete silence."**
>
> *"Although they face the same generic problems as others (low wages, delay of wages, kafala, etc.), domestic workers*

are particularly vulnerable to potentially extreme abuses (ranging from beating, injury, sexual abuse, or death).

Data available through Migrant-Rights.org shows that there are over 2 million migrant domestic workers in Gulf countries. Migrant domestic workers account for 21.9 percent of the total employment in Kuwait; 36.6 percent of the total female workforce in Bahrain; 99.6 percent of all domestic workers and personal assistants in Saudi Arabia, and 20 percent of the total expat workforce in UAE (750,000 domestic workers).

Abuses against migrant workers may include tragic consequences too. Migrant-Rights.org data shows that 56 percent of all suicides in Kuwait in 2013 were committed by domestic workers; 37 percent of suicide cases involved Ethiopian female domestic workers in Saudi Arabia and 700 suicides among Indian migrants in the UAE between 2007 and 2013." (The New Arab: December 06, 2017; Migrant construction workers in Dubai described horrific experiences and inhumane conditions [AFP] Date of publication: December 5, 2017)

Listening to Hossain's story, we can recite the immortal poem "Dui Bigha Jomi" (*My Little Plot of Land*) written by Rabindranath Tagore a hundred years ago. The poem was written about the class division in the rural society of Bengal, and the injustice of the strong over the weak seems to be a factual social image of being exploited by the rulers of all the countries of all time.

Whispers and Wailings

〜

"Alas, in this world, those who have the most want all
And even a king won't stop until he has grabbed everything--big or small!

I said, "Just begging for two mangoes, sir!"
Master said with a grin, "Fellow disguising a saint is a seasoned thief."
When I heard this, I laughed, and tears trailed from my eyes
You the King of saints today, indeed I am a thief!"

Dui Bigha Jomi (My Little Plot of Land)
Rabindranath Tagore

〜

Chapter 9

A Shocking Incident and UAE Visa Ban for Bangladeshi Workers

Hossein told me about an incident that happened several years ago; a Bangladeshi young man used to work as a driver in another house next to his master's. He had been working in that house for a long time. The owner suddenly needed a "maid" for the cooking or the household work and told the driver to arrange a girl from Bangladesh. The young driver enthusiastically recommended his newlywed wife, who was living in Bangladesh at that time, and the owner agreed. The bride was brought from the country for homemaking. They intended that both husband and wife would stay and work together in one house. Such opportunities are not always available; hence they can be called lucky. But their destiny had something else in store for them; the darkness of the new moon came to their fate. After a while, the owner's greedy gaze fell on the newly arrived bride, and he became restless to rape her. One day, he sent the driver away for work and forcibly raped the driver's wife. When the lad returned home after finishing his work outside, he saw his wife sitting on the bed crying. After asking her about the reason for crying, the wife told him all the facts. He burst into anger and grief but could do nothing. Soon after, he sent his wife back to Bangladesh. At the time of parting, he said to his wife, 'I may not see you again in my life, don't think of anything. Just pray for me.'

The driver was waiting for the opportunity to avenge his loss. One day at noon, he got a chance. After bringing the owner's daughter from school, he found that the house was empty. Realizing the opportunity, he also raped the owner's daughter. Needless to say, the consequence was vicious. Living in an Arab country, the same fate that befell an Arab when he raped a girl was also fallen for him. He might have lost his head or still living in a dark cell in Abu Dhabi. Only God knows what happened to him.

~~~

"In the carnival of this world
How many flowers bloom and surrender to gravity
Do we ever talk?
Does anyone ever remember?

Still, the flowers keep blossoming
The birds always sing
They never think anyone
Wants them or not
In the ears of flowers, in the songs of birds

Many words remain unspelled.

How many wicks extinguish
After burning for the whole night?
Incense burns itself
It smells good
Remember in leisure
The story of the lamp, the pain of the incense."

> *Artist: Sabina Yasmin*
> *Lyricist: Mutafizur Rahman*
> *Composer: Satya Saha*

I have observed that the law does not seem to be the same for everyone anywhere in the world with due respect. There is clear discrimination between the law for the rich and the law for the poor. That Bangladeshi young man must not have taken the law into his own hands; he should have taken refuge in the law. But in this world, where lots of people cross the law gap through injustice, many helpless souls often fall into the trap.

Apart from the victims, the ordinary people of Bangladesh think that the people of Arab countries are very polite. There is no injustice over there, and there is no theft, robbery, rape, fighting, and violence. As they say, the grass seems to be greener on the other side, however, there could be reptiles refuging in that grass.

Even the safest known lands could turn threatening.

If you do not believe me, please read the crime section of *http://www.emirates247.com*. Now, read the prominent dailies of

Bangladesh or watch the news on television. You can read or see myriad stories of domestic women workers returning from Saudi Arabia or the Middle East. Many countries globally, including Indonesia and the Philippines, have now stopped sending female domestic workers to the Middle East. Only the so-called 'poor' Bangladesh is still sending domestic workers.

"Slave" workers in Saudi Arabia: We want to go home, enough ill-treatment.

by Sumon Corraya

"Last year, Dhaka and Riyadh signed an agreement to send 120 thousand workers to Arabia. In 2015, 20952 women left for Arabia, but many have already returned. They recounted stories of abuse and threats, domestic slaves by day, sex slaves by night." (Dhaka; Asia News, 02/19/2016)

BRAC's Migration Program head Shariful Islam Hassan said such reports of violence, exploitation, and torture from domestic aides in Saudi Arabia and other gulf countries had prompted Indonesia and the Philippines to stop sending women as domestic workers to this region. *"Bangladesh is still sending female workers to Saudi Arabia for a minimum wage without checking the conditions of their standards of living." (Dhaka Tribune Sunday, November 11, 2018).*

It seems that Bangladesh does not dare to protest against this oppression. The United Arab Emirates' job market, the second-largest remittance sender for Bangladesh, has been closed for several years. In October 2012, the United Arab Emirates (UAE) stopped issuing visas to all Bangladeshis due to fake travel documents, counterfeit passports, and law and order issues. The UAE has about one million Bangladeshi workers, the second-highest number after Saudi Arabia. Despite the global economic downturn, Bangladesh has been able to build a sustainable labor market for the past few years.

> *"The flow of inward remittance jumped more than 18 percent or US $2.80 billion last year (2019), which may partly be attributed to the incentive provided by the government for sending money through official channels. Bangladesh was the third-highest recipient of remittance in South Asia last year after India and Pakistan and the 11th highest recipient globally. Last year, Bangladesh's remittance income hit an all-time high, giving a breather to the country's ongoing foreign exchange crisis."*
>
> *-**The Financial Express:** Remittance: Next largest source of income Shahiduzzaman Khan | Published: January 01, 2020*

On October 03, 2012, Gulf News reported that thousands of Bangladeshis tried to enter the UAE with fake passports. Hundreds of Bangladeshis were arrested for entering the country with illegal documents a few weeks before the visa ban. Many had been seen carrying forged passports and visas.

> **No new UAE visas for Bangladeshis**
> **Suspension is for security reasons and is not a ban, official confirms.**
> **-Published: October 03, 2012, 21:20 By Bassma Al Jandaly, Senior Reporter**
> *"Gulf News learned that there are thousands of cases of Bangladeshi people caught trying to enter the country with forged passports.*

> *Weeks before the visa suspension, hundreds of Bangladeshis were arrested for entering the country with illegal documents.*
>
> *Many were found carrying forged passports and forged visas."*

I have talked to hundreds of Bangladeshis to inquire into this. The opinion of a majority of people is that some corrupt passport officials in Bangladesh issue forged passports to Arakanese Rohingyas. Several Bangladeshi men told me that many of the security guards at the Bangladesh Embassy in Dubai were Pakistani nationals. They treat Bangladeshis inhumanely. Most importantly, in the case of visas, Bangladeshi passports are more acceptable in Eastern countries compared to Pakistani passports. Due to some unlawful elements operating in Pakistan, the entire country has to face the wrath. Therefore, many Arab countries are wary of seeing Pakistani passports and do not want to issue visas easily. Citizens of several countries were barred from working and entering my workplace, Pakistan being one of them. However, it is unfortunate that many Pakistani citizens and Rohingyas from Myanmar illegally collect Bangladeshi passports and work in Arab countries with visas.

Most of the employees of this illegal Bangladeshi passport scam are involved in various misdeeds. There are no illegal activities that they don't do, including drug trafficking, prostitution, human trafficking, and porn CD selling. After being caught by the police, they were found to be Bangladeshi citizens because of their fake passports. Due to these corrupt officials of Bangladesh, the whole country's image has been tarnished today. Saudi Arabia, United Arab Emirates, and several other countries have stopped issuing visas to Bangladeshis. However, there is no reason to think that genuine Bangladeshis do not commit any illegal acts abroad. But their number is comparatively much less. Most of the working class Bangladeshis live a simple, straightforward, and honest life. Their only concern is to keep their family members well-off in the country by earning money.

However, there is another source on Wikipedia about the visa ban for Bangladeshis. According to Wikipedia, the United Arab Emirates stopped issuing visas to Bangladeshis due to Bangladesh's support for Moscow instead of Dubai in the preliminary election of which country was scheduled to host the World Expo 2020. Although Bangladesh voted for Dubai in the second or final round and Dubai was chosen as the host city, in the end, however, the Arab Sheikh's anger did not subside. Dubai, however, denies the existence of a visa ban. Now no Bangladeshi can come to work in UAE. Although the event was anticipated to be held in Dubai on 20 October 2020 but due to the globe-trotting COVID-19 pandemic, it is now rescheduled to 1 October 2021. After being announced the host of World Expo 2020 (postponed to 2021), thousands of construction workers were needed to prepare for it. And instead of Bangladeshis for this construction work, workers started coming from Nepal, Sri Lanka, India, and African countries. It is now uncertain when the ban will be lifted. Saudi Arabia also withheld visas for many years, now introducing a condition that Bangladesh would send thousands of female domestic workers. The future female domestic workers who are willing to come to catch the wild goose in the Middle East remind me of a song by the mystic Lalon Shah:

"O' silly if you don't know your own self how will you know others
If you don't know the way to your own house
You would be get lost.

If you don't know yourself
No matter how much you wander in this world
Lalon says, there is no way in the end."

-Baul Lalon Shah

In tune with the mystic devotee, it is necessary to understand one's own situation and step on the foreign path; otherwise, there will be no way in the end. If you read the newspapers, you can guess the dilemma of those helpless domestic workers. And I have been a close witness to such Whispers and Wailings for the last eight years.

Chapter 10

Facts of Islamic Beliefs

"Hossein, have they ever abused you physically?" I asked him. He simply gritted his teeth (probably recalling the choicest expletives and the pain of battering) and replied that they did things such as slapping, smacking, and kicking; everything. At first, he was beaten a lot; now that the master is living in another house with his youngest wife, the whipping incidents are a little less. Moreover, the juveniles have not aged enough to beat Hossein. Women don't usually come out in front of the male staff. So there is a significant lack of people at home to lay hands on Hossein. I inquired curiously, "Why did your master hit you, Hossein?" Hossein's simple answer was, "When I came to UAE in November 2011, I could not understand their language. If they had ordered me to do something, I would just stand there, not knowing what to do exactly or supposedly would do something else." When Hossein first came to Arabia, he knew nothing of Arabic.

However, he can now speak Arabic quite well. Hossein's madam also talks to Hossein on the phone from time to time about different matters.

Although Hossein calls his madam 'Mother', she does not often come in front of Hossein or talk to him face-to-face. However, she speaks over the phone. Once she asked, "Tell me, Hossein, was it right for your father to marry another young girl as he already has two wives?" Hossein naively replied to his madam, "No, father should not have done it at all at this age." Hossein's Madam's misfortune is that the United Arab Emirates (UAE) follows Islamic Sharia law; the family law passed by Ayub Khan in 1961 does not rule there. About 99% of people in Bangladesh and Pakistan think that the first wife's permission is required to have a second marriage according to Muslim marriage law. The people in these two countries, in most cases, do not even know or believe even when they are told that it is not Muslim law. Now let share what is written in the ordinance of the military powered President Ayub Khan in 1961:

THE MUSLIM FAMILY LAWS ORDINANCE, 1961

(ORDINANCE NO. VIII OF 1961) [March 2, 1961]

POLYGAMY.

6. (1) No man, during the subsistence of an existing marriage, shall, except with the previous permission in writing of the Arbitration Council, contract another marriage, nor shall any such marriage contracted without such permission be registered.

(2) An application for permission under sub-section (1) shall be submitted to the Chairman in the prescribed

manner, together with the prescribed fee, and shall state the reasons for the proposed marriage and whether the consent of the existing wife or wives has been obtained thereto.

All honorable leaders of the government of Bangladesh often say (as far as I know their election manifesto has mentioned), he/she will not make any law that conflicts with the Qur'an and Sunnah. Honorable Ministers, does this law not conflict with the Qur'an and Sunnah? Let's see what the Islamic scholars have to say about this law:

DAWN

<u>Different interpretations of the law on the second marriage</u>

-*Waseem Ahmad Shah March 17, 2014*

"THE Council of Islamic Ideology (CII) in its recent meeting declared that Section 6 of the Muslim Family Laws Ordinance (MFLO) 1961, related to polygamy, was against Sharia."

In the Islamic world, Dar al-Ifta al-Misriyyah, founded in 1895, is considered the first base for fatwas [religious verdicts]. Egypt's Dar al-Ifta is an Egyptian Islamic advisory, justiciary and governmental body established as a center for Islam and Islamic legal research in Egypt. Dar al-Ifta al Misriyyah is considered among the pioneering foundations for fatwa in the Islamic world. Since its foundation, Dar al-Ifta al-Misriyyah has served as a leading institution representing Islam and international law research. Dar al-Ifta al-Misriyyah is one of the pillars of Egypt's religious foundations, others including Al-Azhar Al-Sharif, Al-Azhar University, the Ministry of Religious Grants, and Dar al-Ifta al-Misriyyah. Now let us see what fatwa Dar al-Ifta al-Misriyyah states about second marriage:

> **Question:** *Is the consent of the first wife to a second marriage obligatory?*
>
> **Answer:** *In neither case is the wife's consent necessary. God has given Muslim men the concession to marry more than one wife. Therefore, when a man feels that his circumstances make it desirable or expedient to take another wife, he may go ahead and do so.*

Bangladesh does not follow Sharia law, but this particular law can hurt some people's feelings, especially religious ones. In this country, the religious sentiment is a little more valued than in the Arab countries. After all, nearly 1400 years after the Farewell Pilgrimage, the Almighty has left the vast responsibility of defending the holy Islam to some sentimental people of this subcontinent. In order to defend Islam and Muslims, they often declare 'jihad'. I do not know why they are so worried. Seeing their actions, it seems that Islam is a very fragile religion, and Islam will be destroyed by the words or deeds of some people. On the contrary, looking at their work, it seems that they have challenged the power of Allah.

Of course, those who are sentimental cannot be blamed. They are in various pains. It is difficult to reconcile the Qur'an, Hadith, and Tafsir, and in many cases, what they used to say through tricky or made-up explanations, people followed in simple faith without hesitation. Suddenly some weird atheists arrive from nowhere and are turning everything upside down through their online preaching and writings. Now again, some Hafez and Muftis of the Qur'an have appeared and started creating more problems for the so-called protectors of Islam.

All the misdeeds of the 'hujurs' (Imam; Islamic concept) in the madrasa (religious institution) and maktab (elementary school) are being revealed one after another without any hesitation. The so-called defenders of Islam try to stop them by using insults, threats, and intimidation without going into a healthy debate. Looking at the Hadith (a collection of traditions containing sayings of the prophet Muhammad), it has been found that:

> *"And surely the Bani Israel was divided into 72 groups. And my ummah will be divided into 73 groups. All these groups will be thrown in Hell, except for one group. The Companions asked: Who is that group? The Prophet (peace and blessings of Allah be upon him) said: Those who follow the way of my Companions and me."*
>
> *- {Sunan Tirmidhi, Hadith No. 2641, Al-Mu'jamul Kabir, Hadith No. 7659, Al-Mu'jamul Awsat, Hadith No. 4889, Kanzul Ummal fi Sunanil Aqwal Wal Af-al, Hadith No. 1060}*

Nothing can be stopped by force in the current age of the internet and information super-highways; everyone must understand this. To find out the real facts, now one does not have to go to the library to research the Encyclopedia, Britannica, or thousands of other books and spend years in the quest for the truth. Today, more information can be uncovered in a matter of minutes at home for the benefit of the internet. The entire book collection of Islam, including the Qur'an and Hadith, has reached our hands through mobile phones. If anyone wants to know the truth and facts, they can find out in a few minutes. So no one can go too far with easily made-up things in the name of the Qur'an and Hadith. It is said in verse 9 of the 15th Surah of the Holy Qur'an, Surah Al-Hijr, that:

اْنَّاْنْحَنْ اْنَّلْزَنْرْكْذَل اْن اْوُهَلَنُ وُظِفْذَحَل ٥

"Indeed, we have sent down the Reminder[1], and indeed We will preserve it."

Mohannad Hakim, Ph.D., a research engineer at Ford Motor's Engine Control and Research Innovation Center, says of Surah Al-Hijr that this Surah gives a message of help to believers: God will protect His revelation, His religion, and His faithful servants. So have a leap of faith in God. The surah contains short and inspiring verses that Allah pumps the strength of your faith. It reminds you of the things He has taken on. Although Allah has said that He Himself is the Guardian of Islam, but the 'guardians of Islam in the world' seem to no longer have confidence in the power of Allah. They have come down in the field to defend Islam.

Most of the people I spoke to confessed that they haven't attempted to understand a single page of the Holy Qur'an, and many of them don't know anything except two or four surahs (verses), let alone completing the whole Qur'an. Unfortunately, they are also more prone to emotional outbursts, leading the way to processions, meetings, or arson. In any case, no matter how much the 'hujurs' (Imams, Priests or Clerics) agitate things for the establishment of peace, it is not my subject today; let me return to Hossein's story.

Chapter 11

The Caged Birds

In the year 2016, I used to go to work quite early in the morning. I would leave my room between 5:30 and 6:00 AM. So early in the morning, every day, I saw Hossein standing outside with his master's son and daughter waiting for the school bus. After putting up the boys and girls on the school bus, Hossein entered the kitchen and arranged breakfast. He makes porota (subcontinental layered flat bread), semolina (coarse, purified wheat middling), mahalla (Emirati Date Crepes), etc., every day. After making breakfast for everyone, he comes to his room with some snacks for himself. Hossein has to eat and drink in his own room; he cannot eat inside the house. After breakfast, he has to water all the trees in the yard and do some chores outside. In the meantime, the preparation for lunch begins. Hossein makes biryani and white rice almost every day for the mistress and the children. He has to cook two or four more dishes, including meat, kebabs, chops, and salads. He cooks for himself and the maid separately. The food of the owner and servant is different, and the cooking is separate too. Sometimes he has to run to the store to buy other things as needed. In the Arab world, these small grocery stores are called 'Bakala'.

Most of the shop owners are from the southern Indian state of Kerala. South Indians predominate in trade and commerce here. 27.1% (9.53 million) of the UAE population is Indian; one million have come from Kerala and about half a million from Tamil Nadu. 20% of Indians are involved in white-collar (professional) jobs, and many Indian entrepreneurs have established successful national franchises in the UAE.

Hossein is like a running machine; there is no time to rest. Everything has to be handled alone. Sometimes I wonder if the family members of Hossein can ever feel the value of his hard work.

The 'Hosseins' are making several 'Nandalals' (lazy person) back in their homeland. If one of the family members goes abroad, the rest of the family thinks they no longer have to work hard to earn money. All the responsibility falls on the shoulder of that poor fellow. With the immigrant workers' hard-earned money, the family members buy new mobile phones, laptops, watches, sunglasses, and expensive clothes here in Bangladesh. Indeed, there are exceptions but very few. People never value what they get very easily; their demands never cease. In addition, some licking teams (suckers) in the language of 'Bangabandhu' (Bangabandhu Sheikh Mujib; Father of Bengali nation) push the family members to ask their foreign-settled member for more money.

They don't have the common sense to realize that it is harrowing to earn money abroad. To most people in Bangladesh, abroad means 'a lot of money is flying in the air', and whenever anything is needed, the 'Hosseins' are ordered to 'send money'. Many workers say that they are in a bad mood because they keep receiving calls from Bangladesh asking for more money. We usually ask during the interview, "Have you ever been angry with someone, and if so, with whom and for what reason?" About 90 percent of the answers are; with family and money. No one back home understands where will their family member get extra money from. After receiving the salary every month, almost the whole amount is sent to Bangladesh, leaving a little for themselves. The migrant workers always wonder why their family doesn't save from the amount sent to them, and the family and relatives back in Bangladesh think about what they do with so much money abroad. The poet beautifully describes it in the last stanza of his song "The caged bird was in the golden cage, free bird was in the forest."

"Both birds love each other, yet unable to come close.
Beaks meet through cage gaps, eyes silently connect.
Neither one can express to the other nor console oneself.
Flapping tormented wings, each asks, 'Come close'.
The free bird is afraid, 'I would be captivated and locked'.
Cage bird's anguish, 'Have lost fly-power, my wings are locked'."

Rabindranath Tagore
Translation: Anjan Ganguly

The song's cage birds can symbolize the Hossein's (the expatriate workers) and their family members are flying like the free birds in the forest with cage birds' hard-earned money. Neither side understands the other no one even tries to. Hossein's can't get out of the cage if they even wish to. The only realization that is their ally is "my wings are clipped" by living in captivity for a long time. And when they dream of getting out of the cage, they recognize, like the bird in the cage, "they do not have the power to fly".

A few days ago, I heard about a boy named Amir Hossein. Born in 1971, he moved to Oman at the age of 16 in 1987 for employment after forging his age as 26 in his passport. After living in Oman for ten years, he worked in Abu Dhabi for the next fifteen years. Now he has been working in Qatar for six years. The grind of the world has been dragging him for the last 31 years. In the meanwhile, after two/three years, he usually goes to Bangladesh for two months' vacation. During one such home-country visit, he got married and became the father of two children. I asked him how long he wanted to stay abroad, to which, he replied, 'Children are too young, let them grow up first, and then I will decide to go home.' I'm pretty sure that when they grow up, his kids will never remember their father's sacrifice. As a result, the old age home will be their real address. In the early life, he took care of the brothers and sisters, now of his own son and daughter. If brothers and sisters had become capable of taking responsibility, they would not have to worry about making their children good human beings. Has anyone ever thought of that miserable housewife who sees her husband after two or three years only for a few days? Children are also deprived of their father's affection.

Abdur Razzak, a boy from Kushtia, said he had worked in Dubai for a few years and earned a lot of money and sent it home. So far, he had sent above 10 million (around 110,000 USD); once bought a Toyota car too. He established a business (hotel) in Deira, Dubai in UAE. He hired a manager named Imran (Bangladeshi countryman) to run his business. One morning, Abdur discovered that the 'desi' brother disappeared with 3.6 million BDT (around 42,000 USD) after committing some other misdeeds. Everything was under Abdur's name, so he was caught by the Dubai police. In the end, he was saved by paying a tremendous amount of fine and had to leave UAE instantly. After returning to Bangladesh, he went to Miarhat of Patia district in Chittagong to meet Imran. thereupon reaching, Abdur Razzak became victim to another conspiracy. Imran told him that he still had some money and he would return it. Earlier, Imran had taken money from many locals in the name of sending them abroad. But he could no longer send those people abroad. Taking the opportunity, Imran went to the people from whom he had charged the money and told them that the agent he had paid for those people's visas was now detained at his house. So they should recover the money from that broker. Razzak knew nothing of this.

The locals of Chittagong grabbed Razzak and held him captive in an unknown place to get their money back. They snatched everything from Razzak and started threatening him. Razzak wisely asked for the mobile phone so that he could call and arrange for a refund. He did not know where he was being held. When he got the phone, he came out and called RAB (Rapid Action Battalion) to be rescued. Fortunately, there was one of his acquaintances working in RAB. After being detained in an unknown place for a few days, he was rescued with police and

RAB's help and came back alive. He now works as a gardener in our place of employment (Qatar) to run his family because of the cruel irony of destiny. Like Hossein, he waters trees and grasses under the scorching sun outside at 120 degrees Fahrenheit or 49 degrees Celsius. I have heard many more such stories like Abdur Razzak's and Amir Hossein's. In his poem "Munajat" (Prayer), the national and rebellious poet of Bangladesh Kazi Nazrul Islam appealed about escaping from all this wickedness. The poet's idea is that there is forgiveness for every sin, but there is no forgiveness for immorality:

"Please save me from all the wickedness
Oh God, you are generous.
O, Lord! Keep me away from baseness
No sin is more degraded.
If I am born hundred times and become more sinner,
I shall remain in hell forever and ever,
I know I know that Lord has forgiveness-
But no mercy for baseness."

Poem: Munajat (Prayer)
-Kazi Nazrul Islam

Chapter 12

Hossein's Daily Life

After arranging lunch for everyone, Hossein comes to his hut with the pot of food allotted for him. Entering the room, his first job is to clean his clothes and take a shower. Then one or two other Bangladeshi boys from the next door would bring their mid-day meal items, and they all sit together and finish lunch. I was often invited to have lunch with them whenever he saw me coming from the mosque on Fridays. I could never keep Hossein's request. I saw Hossein wearing the same two shirts (a T-shirt and a half sleeve shirt) and two pairs of pants again and again. While walking in the afternoon, I often saw Hossein's pants and shirt hanging by the window of the outer house, probably left there to dry after he took a shower. I always saw Hossein wearing those two sets of pants and shirts; he would wear one, and the other was cleaned after taking a shower and hung to dry in the heat of the sun. I saw the pants tied with ribbon instead of belts. I never asked if he had any other clothes except those two pairs. So, I and one of my colleagues (Bill), who was staying in the same villa, gave him some of our clothes.

After lunch, Hossein did small chores around the house and rested in his room for a while. But sometimes, he would get called from inside the house, and Hossein had to run there. Needless to say, if he is a little late, maybe he will be beaten again. Most of the time, he was called to buy potato chips and Coke or any other soft drinks from Bakala (shop) for the children. Sitting in an air-conditioned room with the scorching heat outside can arouse children's desire for cold drinks, and there is no blame for that. Hossein is always ready to fulfill their desire like a genie. The boy, a 'Miskin from Miskin country', is hired to always be on his toes, not for any comfort. In the meanwhile, the arrangement of making snacks started. For the evening snacks, he makes singara (snack dish stuffed with vegetables like potato, peas, peanuts, etc), dal puri (spicy snack stuffed with moong beans, etc.) samucha (fried or baked stuffed pastry), chop, sweets, Arabic tea, etc. Sometimes Hossein has to make many snacks together at the command of the master or mistress.

Almost every house here has a large sitting room near the gate outside the main building. In the evening, the landlord gathers with friends and relatives in this area. The 'Majlis' (council) sits in a different house every time. The women usually gathers inside the house, on the days when there is a meeting in Hossein's master's house. During such times, the pressure of making afternoon meals use to be high on Hossein. I used to see him talking to the indigenous boys in the afternoon while watering the trees. From time to time, he would bring *singara, dal puri*, etc., for himself and his friends, and they would all eat and talk together. I always avoided his offer in various ways when he wanted to give some to me on occasions. I used to take the dates because they were fresh from the tree, and I felt a little bad for depriving Hossein of the reward of giving dates according to his beliefs. But *singara, dal puri* is different; they are for him and his friends. Hossein's workload was a little higher than everyone else's because Hossein had to manage both inside and outside the house alone. Others would do any one of the tasks so that everyone could come in front of Hossein's house and gossip in the evening.

On Friday, 5th August 2016, Hossein requested me to take him to a Bangladeshi shop. He wanted to send some money and do some shopping. On Fridays, Hossein's mistress or the children do not usually stay at home; they go to visit the mistress's mother's house. Around 6 pm, I, Hossein, and Hossein's friend Mr. Taibur Rahman (ex BDR) went to Abu Dhabi. We went to Alam Super Market in Zone-1, Al-Wathik Street. There are many indigenous shops, and there is no place to walk on the crowded streets. Everyone came to buy different things on vacations. Hussain and his friend did some shopping for themselves. I purchased a Bangladeshi PRAN mango pickle, *Jhal-muri* (popular street snack made of puffed rice), fried pulses, etc., and a phone jack from an electronics store next door.

On the way back, I showed them around the mosque as we passed Sheikh Zayed Grand Mosque. In 1996, construction began on the mosque, designed by Syrian architect Youssef Abdalki. It took almost 12 years to complete the mosque at the cost of about 545 million USD. Its construction was completed in 2007. The building complex measures 290 by 420 meters (950 by 1,380 feet), covering more than 12 hectares (30 acres).

Currently, this third largest mosque in the world is about the size of four football fields. More than 40,000 people can pray here at the same time. The mosque holds three Guinness World Records; the largest hand-woven carpet, the enormous chandelier, and the world's largest dome. Next to the mosque is Sheikh Zayed bin Sultan Al Nahyan's tomb, the United Arab Emirates' founding father. We all came back at nine o'clock at night.

Sheikh Zayed Grand Mosque

Two days later, on Monday afternoon, Hossein forcibly invited me to his shack when I was leaving for a walk. He cut some of the fruits (cantaloupe and orange) brought from inside the house and served me with utmost care. That was the first time I had witnessed the decaying environment of his shack. There are no doors towards the inside of the house, even no windows. The small room has two single beds, one horizontally and the other vertically set up, two dirty bed sheets, blankets, and pillows. It goes without saying that there is no place to walk in the house. It has a small bathroom and a small air-conditioned unit attached to the wall. Hossein takes his food by spreading out old newspaper sheets in whatever small amount of space is there. However, Hossein entertained me by presenting food on an empty bed. Hossein's ramshackle hut next to the 24-carat gold Swarovski crystal chandelier at the Sheikh Zayed Grand Mosque, as seen two days ago, was a huge mismatch. When I got back home, I gave Hossein several things, including a blanket, bed sheets, and pillow covers. In the poem 'Manush' (Human), the Rebel Poet Kazi Nazrul Islam speaks of equality. The poet, who has fought poverty like Hossein, has seen "Ashraful Makhlukat" (The best of creature) kicked in the chest to make golden Swarovski crystal chandeliers. That is why the rebellious poet has called them a 'group of foolish hypocrites'. The revolutionary poet Kazi Nazrul Islam wrote equality in his "Manush (People)" poetry.

***

"I loathe the humans
Who are those kissing the holy scriptures of Al Koran, Bible, and Vedas
and thus killing themselves
Snatch away those scriptures from them by force
Wiping out those who brought the heavenly words
While the hypocrites are worshipping the holy books, hear me,
you ignorant mass
It is the humans who fostered those scriptures; no sacred book has brought
forth any humans

Despise them as peasants!
Just look keenly and see if Saint Baloram has arrived in the guise of a
peasant
All the prophets were shepherds tending their herds; it is them who took
charge of the radar
And brought in the eternal words, which still exist and shall last forever

*Yet all the holy books and the seats of prayer
Are not as sacred as the tiny body of a single human."*

-Manush (Human) by Kazi Nazrul Islam

Chapter 13

Living Conditions of Migrant Workers

The road in front of our villa I was living in is T-shaped. There is nothing at the other end of the road but an empty dune. Going a little farther to the right, a huge hospital was being built on that field. And after walking a short distance to the left, there is another road to the left (parallel to the road in front of the villa). Along the street leading to the local mosque and next to the mosque a small convenience store (Arabic name 'Bakala'), a small grocery store where Hossein has to visit several times a day. Through Hossein, I got acquainted with almost all the Bangladeshi boys working in that area. Although I was a very insignificant person, everyone had a very high opinion of me because of Hossein. If there were any need for maintenance in my room, they would come and fix it as soon as I called. Bengalis are also predominant in the field of maintenance. They remain so busy in that job that usually they could not be found easily. As a result, my co-worker (Bill), who lived in the next room, would submit a work order to the office and request me to call them if he needed any maintenance. Usually, one maintenance person would take care of many villas in different areas, so it wasn't easy to meet them two or three days prior. But as I was of Bangladeshi origin, they would often leave other work or come after their working hours to fix it. From my long 7/8 years of experience, I noticed that the working-class people always respected those who were a little better off among us and would do anything right away when we asked for something.

Even back in 2012, when I was staying at the Sulafa Tower in Dubai, 14 or 15 Bangladeshis used to work in the maintenance and cleaning department of the 76-story building. I used to call the boy named Rezaul from Noakhali, whom I mentioned earlier, to clean my and other colleagues' apartments from time to time, which would give him an additional income. He also used to sell phone cards to make extra money. Once he asked me to help with his mother's illness; at that time, I had already left Sulafa Tower of Dubai Mariner and moved to Jabel Ali's Garden apartment. So, initially, I was able to help Rezaul with some cash. But after I moved out, I lost contact with him. They used to be open with me and would tell me if they needed anything, and I would tell them if I needed anything to be done. Except for two or four, they would not want to take any tips easily after any work. I tried to please them in various ways.

During Ramadan in 2012, a few days before Eid, I invited all the building workers, and I cooked Iftar and dinner for them myself. I gave them tips as an Eid gift while they left. There were 13 people, including security guards, maintenance, and cleaners, of whom 12 were Bangladeshis and one Pakistani. On the day of Eid, they invited me to their room and cooked *semai* (sweet dish) for me.

My father always used to say, "Honor, respect, devotion, and love cannot be bought in the market; it has to be earned." Yes, I have received a lot of love from those workers in the Middle East in my life. That's why I didn't have to eat the usual American food in the cafeteria all the time. I usually go to work at around six in the morning and have breakfast in the cafeteria. Whenever they saw me, Bengali boys would come and talk about their weal and woe. Every time Fayez, Zahid, Alkas, Harun, Khokon, and many others from that cafeteria used to rush to the table and say, "Sir, for our staff today, mutton has been cooked, or chicken has been prepared. I'm bringing it in a pack so you can eat it for the dinner." I would take it sometimes, and if there were food in the room, I would say no. It is worth mentioning here that according to the contract, their company takes the money for the food and accommodation for their employees from our employer. American food is cooked for Americans, and for the staff, it is cooked as they like. However, there is no obstacle for them to eat American food. Moreover, much of our food is wasted; the leftovers are thrown away as soon as one meal is over. So they can eat any food they want.

> *"Respect is a mirror; the more you show it to other people, the more they will reflect it."*
>
> A.P.J. Abdul Kalam

I used to see Hossein collecting and storing many carton boxes along the boundary wall of the house. Hossein used to collect the folded boxes of paper that we used to throw away. One day, out of curiosity, I asked, "What do you do with those cartons, Hossein?" Hossein answered that he collected them and sold them at the end of the month and earned an extra 30 to 40 dirham per month, about 675 to 900 in BDT (8-10 USD). Hossein buys phone cards to talk to his mother, wife, and children and spends some of the money on himself. In Bangladesh, I used to see our mothers and aunts storing old newspapers, books, pants, shirts, glass bottles, etc. From time to time, the hawker would come to the house for the old things and exchange them for something new. The peddlers never paid cash, just new things in barter of old ones. From then on, my colleague and I, living in the same villa, would not trash any cartons and would call Hossein. However, Hossein also had rivals in this work. Several people in the area collected cartons in the same way and earned some extra money. The rule was, whoever sees the cartoon first, gets to keep it.

Hossein usually did not go out of the area to collect them. No one else interfered with one's collection or takes anyone else's. Once, I dropped several empty boxes of water, and a Pathan boy came and grabbed it and carried those boxes behind his bicycle. When asked, Hossein informed me of his rivalry with his usual smile. Hossein, however, did not have a bike, so he collected the cartons next door. From then on, not only our cartons, but also whenever I walked and saw boxes somewhere, I would stand there and call Hossein, and Hossein would go and collect them immediately.

Gradually my closeness with Hossein began to grow. Almost every day in the dry midday sun or the late afternoon, when we were driving home in an air-conditioned car or relaxing in the cooling air condition of the house, we would see Hossein, wearing his trivial pair of full pants, t-shirt and a towel wrapped around his head, obeying the orders of his master's son or daughter, running like the mailman at the speed of an arrow towards that small grocery store half a kilometer away. By ignoring the scorching heat of the sun of the Middle East, which is followed by blisters on the bare skin of the body, Hossein rushes, sometimes to get a packet of chips, sometimes to bring a can of soda, and sometimes to bring candy. This is an outside job, so Hossein has to do it; there should not be any objections.

People like Hossein are tortured and oppressed everywhere; there is no one to listen to them. That is why they, like a Miller's bull, have been living in silence for the rest of their lives. I have already shared that Hossein had introduced me to many other Bangladeshi boys who work on that street and in all the houses. Some work as gardeners, some as cooks, some as housekeepers, some as maintenance workers, and some as drivers. However, there is an unspeakable pain in everyone's mind. There are stories of their own nightmares. I listened to their history, sitting with thousands of Bangladeshis in Dubai for four years of my life. Many of them came to me and shed tears, and I sat silently listening to their heart-wrenching stories. I have tried my best to alleviate their suffering as much as possible. We forced many companies to change the situation of these boys.

Eid-ul-Fitr was celebrated on Sunday, August 9, 2012. At that time, I lived in an apartment on the 68th floor of the Sulafa Tower in the Dubai Mariners. I would go for a walk in the afternoon at the Marina next door. Next to the clear blue waters of the Laguna are a walkway and a variety of food stalls and shopping centers, some grocery stores in between.

One day, while shopping at a local grocery store, "Spar", I met a Bangladeshi lad Ahsan who came from Khulna. He worked at the "bagging" part of the store, which means, he would put the bought items in the bag at the counter. I used to buy things from there. Before Eid, he cordially invited me to visit his place. He worked till 2 o'clock on Eid day. I promised him I would come. That was my first experience of visiting a labor camp. I went to his room and saw fourteen people living in a small room (approximately 10x12 feet). There was no place to walk. The four bunk beds at the four corners had three beds. each rising from the floor to the top, accommodating a total of twelve people and two more in the empty space on the floor. There was a small bathroom, and cooking was done in a small hut next to the veranda. I have never had the opportunity to visit a prison in any country, but I can imagine that these workers' living conditions are worse than prisoners'. I had to sit on Ahsan's bunk bed with my head bowed, and body bent. There, he served me hot food prepared at night of the Eid day. We had a minimal conversation in the room because one or two people who worked night shifts were sleeping before getting buckling up for their next shift. I ate a little and came back with a completely new, yet bitter experience.

> "Oh Compassionate
> What I wanted and what I got is
> going to lit a lamp for long
> I burned myself
>
> To catch the bird called happiness
> I bought a gold cage by selling everything
> Cutting the gold chain,
> The bird flew away again
> I don't think it was the consequence of that hope."
>
> Artist: Manna Dey
> Lyricist: Pulak Banerjee

Chapter 14

Story of 49 Workers and Bangladeshi Consulate

In 2014, I heard another inhuman story from several people. Their company rented a garage-like space for 49 (forty-nine) people. There was no kitchen, no good bathroom. When they came home from work, they had to take turns cooking on a heating plate. They had to go through the queue if they wanted to use the bathroom. After spending twelve hours working and another two hours of traveling, they came to the room after fourteen hours, had food, and went to bed at about midnight. After sleeping only for three hours, those poor fellows again had to get up early and line up to go to the bathroom. The company bus arrived between four and five in the morning to take them to work. The bus did not have any air conditioning. A medium-sized bus packed with around 50 people and an hour-long ride in the Middle East's sweltering heat is not desirable for a healthy person. Keeping the windows open was not an available option because of desert sandstorms. It's like roasting a living person on slow heat.

There was no way to revolt; the fear of being sent back to the country by canceling the visa was hanging on the head with insults and physical torture. The unfortunate workers had to borrow a lot of money and sell land to come abroad, so they needed to earn money. That was why they endured everything silently without any second option. Those who used to come earlier had to pay the brokers from one lakh seventy to one lakh eighty thousand (170,000 to 180,000) BDT (around 2,000 USD). Those who came later said they had spent three to four lakh BDT (around 4,000 USD). At the end of the month, their salary was 600 to 700 dirham which is only 13500 to 15800 BDT (around 180 USD). If anyone couldn't go to work for one day due to illness, three days' salary would be deducted. Their supervisor and site engineer were both Pakistanis. Engineer Mr. Anwar (from Pakistan) worked as an engineer, but he did not have any engineering degree. As per the CNN report dated 20th June 2020, more than 30% of Pakistani civilian pilots have fake licenses and are not fit to fly. According to Golam Sarwar Khan, Pakistan's aviation minister, in a speech to the National Assembly, 282 of 860 pilots did not sit for the test. They paid someone else to get a pilot's license. So it was surprising but not impossible that Mr. Anwar was working without an engineering degree. Both of them used to torture Bangladeshi workers and favored Pakistani workers a lot.

It should be noted here that the salary of a Bangladeshi certified electrician was 700 dirhams (around 180 USD) per month. The wages of a Pakistani assistant working under him, whether not certified, was 800 dirhams (around 220 USD) per month.

Salary depends on which country you come from, not on the job. We pressured the company to accommodate them well and provide them with new buses and the two officers' dismissal. As a result of our pressure, the workers' condition improved to an extent. The company moved the workers to labor camp from garage and the new bus had an air-conditioner.

Two years back (in 2019), I went to Kuwait for a couple of weeks. Upon reaching there, I learned from interviews of hundreds of Bangladeshis that they had spent an enormous amount of money. Their monthly salary was 60 to 75 Kuwaiti dinars, which is equivalent to 19 to 20 thousand BDT (around 230 USD). They could not save even 10 thousand takas (around 115 USD) because of the cost of living. After sending money to the country for the family's expenses, it takes 6/7 years to pay the agent's loan. They came in search of the gold laying goose by selling land, houses, or borrowing money; but they had not recovered any of the pledged belongings. Upon entering the airport, the passport was taken from them so that no one could escape. Even if there is a way to escape, the practice is closed; the family is in debt of millions. Alas, the self-proclaimed foreigner, when I look at them, I am reminded of the song of Late Andrew Kishore:

"Whom shall I explain the distress?
I'm heartbroken
There is an incessant fire burning inside slowly."

Lyrics: Radharomon
Music: Bidit Lal Das

As mentioned earlier, Indians, Nepalese, Sri Lankans, or Filipinos are in a much better position. None of them spent more than 60 to 70 thousand in their currency. Moreover, the embassies of those countries are quite active, especially the Indian embassy. If there is any difficulty in the work or if the salary is not paid up to the standard, help is received from the embassy. They maintain regular contact with the concerned government and the Labor Department.

Mr. I.A., the founding president of the Bangladesh Business Council in Qatar, mentioned an incident to me in this regard. He works at a high rank for a well-known company here. Mr. I.A. said that ambassadors from various countries posted in Qatar met him and the company's head to discuss how to do business in Qatar or with his company. The CEOs of the various corporations in Qatar were invited to the ambassadors' various events for public relations. Mr. I.A. also went to all those events as a guest. The ambassadors discussed in detail the benefits of investing in their country, the services offered to investors, or how to bring their country's business to Qatar. They even collected information on how to bring skilled workers from their homeland. Mr. I.A. further said that he had personal phone numbers of at least 30/35 ambassadors to keep in touch with him or the chairman of his company; they answer every time he calls for any work. The most significant thing he mentioned that he had been in the country for more than 14 years, and to date, no Bangladeshi ambassador or any of his staff had gone to his office or to pay a courtesy call to the head of his company. Once at a function at the Indian Embassy, the Indian Ambassador introduced Mr. I.A. to the Bangladeshi Ambassador. Where to hide the shame? You have to get acquainted with the Ambassador of your own country through the Ambassador of another country!

Earlier, I heard in Dubai that the Ambassador has to go to the airport for at least 3/4 days a week to serve any VIP coming from Bangladesh or transiting through the airport. Dubai and Qatar are two places that are the main hubs of international aviation or the center of east-west communication. There are so many VIPs running through all these routes that the Ambassador is always busy entertaining them. In such a scenario, where is the time to pay attention to the plight of ordinary workers? That is why it seems that Nachiketa Chakrabarti (Kolkata) has come up with an easy way to settle the child's life through his songs with sarcasm:

"What more I can say about my child so dear
Not a doctor, not a lawyer
I will make you a minister."

Singer: Nachiketa

Chapter 15

The Contribution of Middle Eastern Workers to the National Economy

One day I asked Hossein, "Hossein, what dishes can you cook?" Hossein replied with a usual laugh, "I can cook everything, sir." He cooks biryani for lunch every day for the master's family. Being a little surprised, I asked, "Do they eat *biriyani* every day for lunch?" Hossein replied, "Yes, sir." Apart from this, *porota* and *meat* for breakfast, *luchi* (deep-fried flatbread), *singara,* etc., for the afternoon snacks; any other item for dinner. "Hossein, can you cook fish?" Hossein answered with delight, "Yes sir, I can." I said to Hossein, "If I buy you fish, will you be able to cook fish for me one day?"

Hossein gladly replied, "Sir, give it to me on Friday. No one stays at home that day. I will cook." On Friday morning, Hossein's madam used to go to her mother's house. The children do not stay at home either, and they go to different places. And the master lives in a separate house with his younger wife in another area. Only Hossein and the maid stay at home. He also told me about which store had the best tilapia fish. Bengali lives for 'fish and rice', so I could not forget the taste of native fish despite staying abroad for 35 years. Occasionally, I want to eat fish. As he had affirmed, I bought some tilapia fish on Friday morning and asked Hossein to cook two for me and keep the rest for himself and his friends. At lunchtime, I saw Hossein appeared with two or three pots; one with fish, one with rice, and one with dal (lentil). I asked him, "What have you done? I just bought fish to cook, I already brought rice from the cafeteria, and I didn't buy you pulses or asked you to cook. Who will eat that much food now?" Hossein smiled and said, "Sir, I can cook delicious lentils; it's lip-smacking. No problem, you keep eating slowly. I will come later and take the pots."

Hossein did not fabricate this statement at all, as his cooking is really excellent. After a long time, I had local food (fish) with so much pleasure. In the evening, when Hossein came to fetch the pots, I thanked him and wanted to give him some money. However, as I offered him money, seeing Hossein's condition, it seemed that he would die in shame. "Sir, I consider you as my elder brother. How could you think I will take money from you for cooking a day's meal? No problem, whenever you want to eat Bangladeshi food, I will cook it if you tell me." I thought to myself that this shame is not of Hossein; this shame is of all of us who live in high seats. Some of us steal orphans' money; some people embezzle hundreds of thousand takas, promising Hossein's a good life abroad, forcing them to sell their homesteads. Some falsely marry and bring ordinary village girls into the city and then sell them for prostitution or trafficking abroad. Some hire street children to set fire in a moving bus with petrol bombs and kill people. I don't know how much money a person has to make to quench his thirst.

Today I have suddenly remembered an incident of our great liberation war of 1971. I was a fifth-grader then. On 27th March, the brutal Pakistani army lifted the curfew from Kushtia city for some time. I was going to cross the Gorai River with my family and take shelter in the village. The boat was filled with town folks. Everyone was fleeing from the city to some rural areas possible. Panic was hula-hooping everywhere because if the Pakistani army spotted us, they would shoot. All were trying to cross the river and reach a safe distance inside the village as fast as possible. In that horrible moment, I witnessed something that is still afresh in my memory drive. The village's ordinary people were serving the frightened people of the city with some food (muri, chira, molasses, coconut, etc.) on the side of the road, pouring out all the love of their hearts. Everyone asked the same question: What was the city's condition, how many people have been killed, have all the houses been burnt down? Looking across the river, you could see black smoke snaking towards the city sky. On the way, the villagers were requesting the escapers to take a rest at their houses. If anyone had no place to stay, the courteous villagers would leave their bedrooms and take their children outside to the veranda. What an exemplary deed of humanity! The poet may have written by seeing people like them:

"This bond that tugs, rivals love for a brother or mother,
I yearn we not separate but stay together forever,
This land that nourished me from birth,
How I wish this as the place of my final breath on earth.

Nowhere else a place of such luminous glories,
This is the Queen of all lands on earth,
This is the land of my birth, the hallowed land of my birth."

Lyrics: Dwijendralal Roy
Translation: Zakariya Mohiyuddin

After independence, the real face of the town folks began to emerge. Their gentleman-like masks didn't last long after then as the situation was entirely different, and there was no need for shelter. That was why they would cover their faces with an umbrella seeing the peasants of the village from a distance on the road. It cannot be said if those farmers would want a favor to visit their home. If anyone finds out that the shelter seekers took refuge in their home during the war, then it is a matter of prestige. So the elite class who took refuge in the villages could not associate with villagers who offered shelter. In the post-war period, these elite class people became the heads of society, grand warriors, social workers, and partners in their state power. Those simple people of the village had nothing to ask for. They have silently served the country and the people. Without their silent support in 68,000 villages of Bengal, it would have been almost impossible for the freedom fighters to wage guerrilla warfare. Bangladeshi heroic warriors fought with the brutal Pakistani army and took refuge in these unknown and ordinary people's homes. These people prepared hot meals for the warriors in the middle of the night with what they had in the house; they often slaughtered their chickens and lambs. The mistress of the house would cook hot supper, and the men of the house stayed up all night guarding our weary great heroes. Their stories have been written in very few books in the history of Bangladesh. Even today, no government has recognized these allied freedom fighters yet. Veteran MP (Member of Parliament) Late Suranjit Sen Gupta once said in a speech in Parliament to list the '*Rajakars*' (traitors) instead of the freedom fighters because everyone outside the '*Rajakar list*' was a freedom fighter.

Throughout the ages, the Hosseins have been born in our country to serve others selflessly. Many of today's fighters, whome we ignorantly call *'Kamla of the Middle East,'* have been fighting to keep the economic wheel of the country and family afloat by sacrificing their happiness.

Year	KSA	UAE	Qatar	Oman	Kuwait	USA	UK	Malaysia	Singapore	Italy	Others	Total (in million USD)
2018-19	3110.40	2540.41	1023.91	1066.06	1463.35	1842.86	1175.63	1197.63	368.33	757.88	2241.47	16,419.60

Source: Bangladesh Bank

Today's largest share of Bangladesh's 35 billion dollars in foreign exchange reserves comes from these neglected Middle Eastern workers' remittances. There are many wealthy Bangladeshis in Europe and America, and very few send money to the country. On the contrary, in many cases, they send money to foreign countries from Bangladesh. There may be some exceptions, but the number is negligible. It can be said that 100% of the Middle Eastern workers send money back home, but 100% of the European-American Bangladeshis do not send money back. According to Bangladesh Bank, of the 16.42 billion dollar remittances in the 2018-19 fiscal year, only 3.78 billion (23%) came from the United States, the UK, and Italy. The remaining 12.64 billion (77%) came from the hard-working Hosseins'.

It hasn't been long since the day when, in the house of a man called *'Bon Kheko'* (forest eater), billions of illegally earned Bangladeshi currency was found inside drums, inside the mattress, the pillow, even in the trash. I read in the newspaper that his mother and sister were living in the village with incredible difficulty. Even then, I hear that their addiction to making money does not go away. Bill Gates, one of the richest men in the world, has been donating his wealth to the Bill and Melinda Gate Foundation to serve the poor, the Nobel laureate Mother Teresa and President Barack Obama have spent all their prize money on charity. On the contrary, the prize money from Nobel Prize in Bangladesh is spent on funding the US presidential election. What a strange country and a nation! Like the poet said, *"You will never find such a country anywhere."* Honestly, it's hard to find such a country in the world. The first people to come to our home after 9/11 with a message of courage were the members of a local church. They apologized for the small number of incidents across the United States and gave us their personal number to call whenever needed. When I went for the prayer on Friday, I saw that the whole mosque was surrounded by police and the FBI members so that nothing wrong could happen. Shortly after the prayers, the police chief, the FBI, a member of the local city council, and the church's priest said in a speech that they would not tolerate any anarchy and call them immediately in case of any disruption. They are following Zero Tolerance. I had seen the same thing happen again before the last presidential election in 2016 because the then-presidential candidate, President Trump, said something anti-Muslim. The FBI official made it clear that the FBI does not follow any political party or rhetoric; they look at people of all parties, all religions, and all castes in the same light. There is no room for discrimination here. The local police chief and the priest of the local church also shared the same views.

After the Babri Mosque demolition on 6 December 1992, how many Imams or clerics or Bangladesh have come to the houses of traditional religious (Hindu) people with a message of courage, or how many police officers have covered the Buddhists with a safety blanket during the Ramu incident on 29 September 2012? Yet most Muslims think Islam is the best religion in the world, and Muslims are the people of the best nation. Islam is the religion of peace, so Muslims can give cold shoulder to countries like America to establish peace. Muslims think that they will go to heaven one day, and Non-Muslims are infidels, faithless; they will never find the pleasure of the heavens. Here lies the consolation. In interviews, many have told us that they would not like to work with Americans or pagans. When asked about allegiance to any country, their answer goes directly in favor of Saudi Arabia. My American colleagues wondered why they were not loyal to their homeland Bangladesh but loyal to Saudi Arabia? Going further, he was asked, will you take up arms for Saudi Arabia? "Of course, Saudi Arabia is a Muslim country," he replied without a doubt in his mind. Many of those who have studied in madrassas have said that in madrassas in some particular areas, physical exercises, using sticks, wielding swords, and wielding weapons are taught. Many madrasas have a teacher named 'Jihadi Huzur' who teaches these to the students and inspires them to go for jihad. Yes, this information is all stored with different agencies.

I don't know how much the image of Bangladesh is maintained through the information mentioned by them. No rules of the Bangladesh government are followed there (in madrasas). Most of their money comes from different Middle East countries and funds are raised from other sources by using these children from the madrasa. Needless to say, the US government takes account of this information provided by them and analyzes the trial very seriously. Alerts are issued by the State Department only when similar information is revealed from different agencies. As a result, we had an extra responsibility to be ultra-careful with the madrassa students from those areas. In the end, the situation was such that if it is seen in the interview that someone has come from a madrassa, special care has to be taken about them. About 95% of Bangladeshis who come from madrassas are anti-US, and almost all of them are also anti-Bangladesh government as well. Talking to them, what I understood was that most of them think of the current Bangladeshi government as "anti-Islamic atheist" and "India's puppet". So there is no room for complacency of the government. Religious tolerance should be increased enormously.

"If time passes by, there would not be any achievements
(physical or spiritual)
Why did you not pursue when you had the time?"

-Lalon Shah

The famous Leiden University of the Netherlands published a research paper in this regard in 2019. The university is ranked in the top 100 universities in the world by three significant statistics. It is ranked among the top 50 in the 2020 QS World University Rankings in 13 different categories: Classical and Ancient History, Politics, Archeology, Anthropology, History, Pharmacology, Law, Public Policy, Religious Research, Arts and Humanities, Linguistics, Modern Languages, and Sociology. So any research paper published by this university can be believed without a doubt.

PERSPECTIVES ON TERRORISM

Volume 13, Issue 5   October 2019

Profiles of Islamist Militants in Bangladesh by Shafi Md Mostofa and Natalie J. Doyle

"Since the early 1980s, Bangladeshi militants have joined wars in Libya, Palestine, Afghanistan, Iraq, and Syria to fight for what they defined as the Ummah. Foreign cases of perceived Muslim suffering have always played a significant role in the escalation of Islamist militancy in Bangladesh. Originally, violent Islamists emerged principally in the Madrassas and came from poor families with rural backgrounds."

Recently a research book written on madrasas was banned by the government. I haven't read the book yet, but there is no criticism of religion in the book from what I have learned from various sources. Only that many real incidents of child rape in mosques and madrasas are mentioned in the book. This cannot be the reason to ban a book. It may be mentioned here that on page 43 of the book "Prison Diaries", a book written by Bangabandhu Sheikh Mujib (Father of the Nation)' and published by Bangla Academy under the direct supervision of Honorable Prime Minister, the Father of the Nation Bangabandhu has mentioned that:

> *"In the afternoon, I came across a Maulana-a Hafiz, that is to say, someone who knows the Qur'an by heart; his father was a famous pir or saint of Comilla district. He would give a speech before the start of prayers and then a sermon in the middle of it; the convicts would listen to him all the while. I listened to his speech from afar on this occasion. He then said, "Recite the Durud Sharif loudly, and the verses will drive away Satan. Read it as loudly as you can." He then discoursed at great length. He was good-looking, young, and had a compelling way of delivering the speech. But the cloth he wore was very large-sized. That was what made me suspicious. It stretched to his feet and must have been six or seven yards in length. He had a rosary bead in his hand. From time to time, he would close his eyes as he discoursed.*
>
> *I inquired about finding out what case had been lodged against this Maulana (Imam). One of the guards here told me, "Don't you know? He has been accused of rape! He used to teach Qur'an a girl student and had forcibly abused her right inside the mosque. The girl was 11/12 years old, and when she screamed, people came inside the mosque and discovered what was going on. They then got hold of the Maulana and gave him quite a beating. He had to be admitted to the prison hospital for a while after he had been brought to jail." I said, "And now that he is in prison, he has begun preaching again!" What an imposter! He has been putting on quite a show.*

After dusk, we were locked in. The Hafiz (who memorizes the Holy Qur'an) was being stationed on the floor above where I was in. After the early evening prayer, he conducted a Milad (preaching) session, then recited verses, and then held a discussion session. It seemed to me that he was out to show everyone how adept he was in the Qur'an and how he had mastered it by heart. However, he had been proved guilty in the case lodged against him and sentenced to four years of prison. He had applied for "division". On inquiry, it was found out that he was from a reputed family. However, he was denied bail because he had been convicted of using brute force."

Bangabandhu is describing this incident of 1949. From here, it is understood that even then, the Hafez or Maulanas of the mosques were acquiesced for rape, and for that, they had faced strict punishments, didn't even get division. And now the mention of these incidents hurt the feelings, and a book is banned. I have some real experience with the banning of books. The author, Salman Rushdie, became famous overnight when Iran issued a death sentence for his book "Satanic Verses", written in the late 80s. Before that, very few people even knew his name. At that time, I was working at Dallas-Fort Worth International airport. One day, when I went to work, I saw that one of my colleagues Muhammad Zubayer, an Ethiopian Muslim, had picked the book off the shelf and started reading it. Talking to him, I came to know that he knew nothing about the book or that he had no interest in buying it. It is only that since there is so much fuss about that book, he bought it. Needless to say, the book has sold about 0.8 million copies.

Every time I have visited Bangladesh in the last 40 years, I use to return with two suitcases of books from Bangladesh.

My collection contains thousands of books in my home in the United States. In 1993, when Bangladesh's government banned the book "Lajja" (Shame) written by Taslima Nasrin, I was looking to buy it. Suddenly I discovered that the book was already on my shelf. Every time I buy a book, I make time and keep reading. At that moment, I was reading another book. So, I postponed reading that and finished reading the book "Shame" first. It is worth mentioning here that very few authors sell 50,000 copies of books in Bangladesh, but the book "Shame" surpassed that record long ago.

In the nineties, the legendary subcontinent singer Lata Mangeshkar came to Dallas, Texas, to perform in an event. The performance was on Saturday, and the local mosque announced that it was haram (forbidden) for the Muslims to attend the ceremony. It was a charity show for establishing a Hindu Temple, so it was forbidden to go there. I witnessed another such incident during the US presidential election in 2000. The 2000 presidential election was one of the most controversial elections in US history. In that election, Mr. Albert Gore received 51,003,926 popular votes across the United States, and Mr. George W. Bush received 50,460,110 votes. Mr. Gore received 48.38% of the total vote, and Mr. Bush received 47.87%. But Mr. Gore received 266, and Mr. Bush received 271 electoral votes (49.4% Gore and 50.4% Bush). It is noteworthy that Mr. Gore was also ahead in the electoral vote before the Florida vote was added (Gore: Bush - 266: 246). But Florida reversed the overall result with just a difference of 537 votes. In this state, Mr. Gore received 2,912,253 votes, and Mr. Bush received 2,912,790 votes. The "defenders of Islam" played a vital role in changing the image of the option here. Since Mr. Gore's nominated VP, Joseph Lieberman was a Jew; it was preached in the mosques not to vote for Mr. Gore. The Muslim population in South Florida was estimated to be between 90,000 to 110,000. Of those, if 1% voted for Mr. Bush following the mosques' preach, at least 900 to 1,100 votes went against Mr. Gore. As I said before, Mr. Gore lost in Florida by just 537 votes. The result of electing Mr. Bush as President was soon felt by the sentimental friends.

I have described the events here because banning a book means making that book and the author famous overnight. In the current era of information superhighways, it is not possible to hide anything. People's interest in any forbidden thing is usually a little higher by birth. Only open discussion without a ban can solve this problem. For example, US TV stations such as CNN, NBC, ABC, and CBS have been criticizing the government almost all the time, but to date, I do not know of any TV channels that have been shut down for this reason. This is a real example of democracy.

One thing needs to be said here in context. The first time I lived in Dubai Marina in the UAE back in 2012, I could not hear any 'azan' (call for prayer) in the morning. One of the imams of that country was officially forbidden to give a ring to Fajr prayers (a Muslim prayer offered to God at the dawn hour of the morning) in the area in the morning because many foreigners live there and are the guests of that country. Their sleep should not be disturbed in the morning. Today the time has come for our self-criticism.

*"When the world is moving forward
We're still stationary,
Seeking fatwa for divorcing wife
Searching through fiqh and hadith.*

*Hanafi, Shafi'i, Maliki, Hambli
It has not been sorted out yet,
At that time, Azrail came
Shouted, let's go.*

*As much as I died on the outside
Replicated on the inside too,
We are growing in number
Like cows and goats."*

— Kazi Nazrul Islam

Chapter 16

The Hypocrisy of the Bangladeshi Elite Class

With the workers' sweat and blood-soaked earnings like Hossein's, paid only 900 dirhams per month, Bangladesh Bank's reserve currency has exceeded 35 billion dollars. How much can those of us who live in higher seats contribute to that 35 billion? I coined this as 'blood money'. But the government does not invest in persons likes Hossein. Such ill-fated souls step towards unknown destinations, sell their houses, lands, or deposit through brokers, spending millions of money on loans. In most cases, it takes three to four years to repay. The people I spoke to earlier said they came here after paying one and a half to two hundred thousand BDT to the broker to catch the Middle East's wild goose. Those who came later had to spend four to five hundred thousand BDT on the broker.

It is worth mentioning here that the workers' company has to abide by several rules including salary, living conditions, and weekly working hours for those who come to work for us. However, there are no signs of such guidelines at work, as companies would hire workers of their choice and pay them as little as possible. The companies are almost 100% Arabic-owned, but Egyptian, Palestinian, Indian, Pakistani, Filipino, and Nepalese dominate the management. There are some Europeans or Americans on the leadership panel, but there is a small handful of Bangladeshis. Egyptians and Pakistanis are at the forefront to abuse, torture, beat, and provide low pay. Even Indians pay less, but they swear or abuse very little. In all cases, the norm to pay the monthly salary on time is not maintained. If someone cannot go to work for one day due to illness, three days' salary gets deducted. All the rules are strict for Bangladeshis only; Pakistanis or Indians deduct one day's wage for a day off for workers in their companies. After two to three years of continuous work within a work contract, they get 30 to 40 days' leave to go home. Many of them do not want to go to their homeland so that they can earn some extra money. I have heard from many people that they do not go to their country for 8/10 years. According to them, only Europeans and Americans pay more money and pay the salary on time, on the first day of the month.

It is unbelievable but true that by smuggling this blood money sent by the unfortunate workers, elite classes are building houses on a human-made island, Palm-Jumeirah, in the middle of one of the world's most expensive seas in Dubai; spending tons of money abroad for treatment, while the Hossein's are destined for a community hospital. The elite class might be spending billions of cash abroad on vacations; sending their children to foreign educational institutions instead of domestic universities to maintain the status. No one takes the headache to improve the domestic universities as the sons and daughters of the people who lift the society are studying abroad. Who keeps track of how many students' futures are being tarnished after being stuck in Bangladesh for years on session jot? A few days ago, I watched on the news that the students were protesting in the streets for the test result given a year ago. Unfortunately, only these Hossein's, when they go to their homeland for a vacation after two-three years, face difficulties in every step starting from the airport. Almost everyone looks down on them as 'Middle Eastern Kamla' (toiler of the Middle East).

Hossein used to wash the cars of some people at night to make some extra money. When everyone was asleep, he and his friend (Taibur Rahman) would clean three or four vehicles together. In the Middle East, often there are sandstorms. The cars need to be cleaned every one or two days. Most people hire someone on a monthly basis to clean their vehicles. Hossein had to wash the cars of his master but did not get paid extra money for it. After renting the vehicle, I also told Hossein to wash the car two days a week. At first, he objected to taking money from me, but I did not listen and insisted on paying him for his service. I told him that there was no need to clean the car if he didn't take the money; in the end, he agreed. Thus, when everyone fell asleep in the dark of night, Hossein kept the cars clean for extra income. By cleaning the car in this way, Hossein would make a couple of hundred dirhams extra. Occasionally, while washing the car at night, the housemaid Taslima would see and threaten him that she would tell the owner. To disarm her, Hossein used to do a lot of work for the housemaid like an obedient person.

One day, I asked Hossein what he would do if he got sick or needed to see a doctor. Does he have any health insurance? This, however, is the rule of the government in this country.

> *"The Health Insurance Law of Dubai No11 of 2013 requires that all Residents must have a level of health insurance that meets or exceeds minimum benefits stipulated by Dubai Health Authority (DHA).*
>
> *In Dubai, employers are legally obligated to provide medical cover for their employees. Article 10, section 2 states that employers must not deduct premiums or reduce the employee's salary to mitigate insurance cover costs. The law also states that all dependents (this includes spouse and children) and domestic workers (including maids, cooks, drivers) of the employee must also be covered for basic health insurance. This basic health insurance is called the Essential benefits plan (EBP)."*

Hossein's master has made a government hospital card for Hossein. If he has to see the doctor, he goes to the government hospital in Abu Dhabi by bus or taxi. It is quite a luxury for Hossein to go by taxi. It goes above 50 dirhams (around 15 USD) to travel. Then there is also the co-pay cost of doctors and medicine. Hossein's master never takes Hossein to doctors or pays him any money for treatment. So, all the expenses have to be borne by Hossein, and the only way to save money in an ill-condition is traveling by local bus. He has to go to the hospital and stand in line for registration. If he doesn't go very early in the morning, standing in a long line is time-consuming. Then comes waiting at the doctor's office with the registration ticket.

If another test (blood test, X-ray, etc.) is needed to be done, separate registration in a different line is required. Moreover, if the doctor gives a prescription, going to the pharmacy and collecting the medicine, again, by standing in a serpent-like queue is a must. All in all, visiting a government hospital once means a whole day goes for a toss.

On Friday, August 26, 2016, Hossein once again wanted to go to Abu Dhabi for some work. Mr. Taibur Rahman (Hossein's friend) also went with us that day. As Eid ul Adha was in two weeks, it was crowded. I could not find a parking space, so I waited in the car, and they came back after completing the work. On the way back that day, we went to visit the Dalma Shopping Mall. The mall is located in the town of Musaffah. It is about fifteen kilometers away from the area where we lived. Musaffah is a suburb of Abu Dhabi. Most of the residents around here are from the Indian subcontinent. Lots of Bangladeshi people also live in this area. Hossein had never come to this shopping center or mall, although he lives nearby.

None of them have had the good fortune to see such an expansive mall before. The mall has three floors. As we walked across the branded stores, I noticed Hossein relishing the grandeur without blinking an eye, like a curious kid. That day I bought a wireless keyboard, mouse, and a floor lamp from the mall. Hossein did not allow me to carry any of the packages. He lugged things in his hand and walked around the mall with me. Then we went to the food court where I ordered food at a Mediterranean restaurant. After sitting in the restaurant, seeing the ambience, it seemed that they felt extremely ashamed. They repeatedly said that it would have been better to eat in a cheap Bengali restaurant than to dine in this expensive restaurant. But then suddenly, they became silent. The three of us didn't talk to anyone on the way home after dinner.

I don't know what was hovering over their minds, but I was reminded of my debt burden. Thirty-six years ago, I set foot abroad with 1,300 dollars of hard-earned foreign currency from Hossein's ancestors. That loan has not been repaid even to this day when I am writing this. Even before that, when I was studying at the famous Dhaka University, known as 'the Oxford of the East', I once heard that the tuition fee we pay was equal to the sum of three days' expenses of the university; these Hosseins paid for the remaining 362 days. That debt also has not been repaid yet. In the "Coolie Mojur" (laborers) poem, the rebellious poet compares these people to Gods. The poet also admits that we have a lot of debt incurred day by day, and it is time to repay that debt to the Hosseins.

"The debt will have to be repaid as it has spiraled day by day
Those who tore the mountains apart with hammers, crowbars, and gads
It is their bones scattered on the sides of the road
They became laborers, and porters to service you
Those who dirtied their holy bodies with dust to carry you,
They are the humans; they are Gods for whom I sing."

- *"Coolie Mojur" by Kazi Nazrul Islam*

Chapter 17

Eid-ul-Adha

The following Monday, on September 12, 2016, it was Eid-ul-Adha. Hossein rarely gets his salary on the set date of any month. That time also, it was not a different story. Eid had arrived, but he had not got the last two months' salary. His ever-smiling bright face sometimes looked pale to me. Upon asking him, I got to know that he was tensed as he did not have any money to send for his children to celebrate Eid.

Meanwhile, it had been more than three years; Hossein had not gotten any leave and could not visit Bangladesh to see his family. Hossein's wife, mother, son, and daughters repeatedly requested him to visit home. According to the terms of his job, he should get leave after every two years. He was keenly planning to celebrate Eid in his own country that year, but unfortunately for Hossein, there is no money and vacations. His employer is afraid that Hossein may quit his job if he gets the complete salary at once. When Hossein asked the employer's spouse about the salary, she repeatedly gave the same answer, 'I don't know, your master knows.' And when he talks about vacations, he gets the response, 'Hossein, what do you want? Let your mistress not eat? If you go on vacation, who will cook and feed us?' So it was a big problem for him. That time as well, Hossein decided to act big-heartedly again, forgetting his own needs for the sake of others; he chose his mother, wife, son, and daughter as his sacrifice. Of course, Hossein may leave his job, but he stops thinking about that fear of an uncertain future.

I asked almost every day, have you got the salary? Hossein's answer was the same, 'Father has not returned yet.' On September 10 Saturday, two days before Eid, I brought Hossein to the room after the afternoon walk. I gave him a new shirt I had bought from the mall for him as an Eid gift and some dirham (UAE currency) in the envelope. He was so happy as if the clock was ticking the best moments for him! He didn't even wait till Eid; the next day, he started wearing the shirt and showed it to everyone. He also called his mother back home. His mother also talked to me on the phone and prayed heartily; I felt a little uncomfortable.

~~~

"Allow me to touch your feet,
Please, please do not step back.
Offering my life and death, my happiness and sorrow –
I shall embrace your feet on my chest.

Ever thirsty desire pain
My desires that are complete disarray –
Please do not scatter them all,
Reconstruct them in a garland.

Annihilate disappointments of my wishes
Undone and ever thirsty,
It must come out triumphant at last –
Defeated by you.

I can't bear anymore moving door to door
Exchanging my poverty,
I may belong to you; please accept me,
Offering me your majestic welcome-garland."

Rabindranath Tagore
- Translated by Anjan Ganguly

I could not do much for Hossein. I asked him, "Don't your madam or father give any gifts or bonus on Eid?" Hossein replied with a smile, "They don't even want to pay the salary properly." Suddenly, on the night before Eid, on the 11th, at around 8 pm, he knocked at the door of my room. I asked him what had happened, and he said, "Sir, my master has just paid my salary. Can you take me to the money exchange in the city by car? I want to send the money home." I quickly got ready and took him to the town to UAE Money Exchange. I asked him in the car if he received the two month's salary? Hossein replied that he had got only one month's salary. After sending all the money to his family, he got relieved. I asked Hossein, "Tomorrow is Eid, will your family get this money before Eid?" Hossein was fortunate that the famous "National Moon Sighting Committee" of Bangladesh always makes some delay in finding out the moon, so Eid is still celebrated in Bangladesh one day after the Middle East. This way Hossein got one more day.

Everyone in Hossein's master's house had gone to meet their relatives to celebrate Eid; they would stay there for a few days. Only Hossein and the working girl (Taslima) were at home. I asked him what he would do on the day of Eid as he had sent all the money and not kept even a penny for himself. He replied with his usual signature smile that he has got some bucks in his hand by selling paper boxes and washing the cars. With that money, he had planned to go out with his friends for a long drive, and in the afternoon, they would have diner together at any Bangladeshi restaurant. After that, they would return home by hiring a taxi. Hossein offered me to accompany them, but as some of my friends who live in Dubai and Sharjah had already invited me for Eid, so I had planned to go there.

Last time, I stayed for four years in Dubai and got the scope to be friends with several families. I have spent a lot of time with them in well and woes. They helped me come out of my loneliness in Dubai. That time, almost every weekend, I would go to one or the other house and gossip about the country, people and eat delicious Bangladeshi food cooked at their home. Sometimes on long weekends, we would go out together for a picnic at the mountain pads or by the sea somewhere far away. I used to go out in the morning and return in the evening after partying throughout the day. Living apart from my own family, my life memories in that foreign land with Mr. Sheikh Abdul Karim (Suja), Saifur Rahman, Mohammed Rabi (Munir), Ikramul Chowdhury, and a few other families will remain precious to me forever. I still have that relationship with them, but this time when I had planned to visit them on the occasion of Eid, the situation was a little different. The last time I lived in Dubai, everyone was reasonably close. But now, my stay had been arranged near the workplace in Abu Dhabi.

So it was no longer possible to go every week just like the last time. Once I go to see them, they wouldn't let me return the same day. I would spend the rest of the night at brother Shuja's house and back to Abu Dhabi in the morning. I promised to spend time with them on Eid, so I did not get the scope to enjoy the festival with Hossein.

Eid prayers are performed here very early in the morning, immediately after the Fajr prayers. I got up in the morning, took a bath, got ready, and went to the mosque for Eid prayers. All Eid congregations are held here in the mosques. In Bangladesh, I have seen even the most important roads in Dhaka remain closed on Friday for the Jummah prayers. But here, it is strictly forbidden to offer prayers in the parking lot, outside the mosque, or by closing the road. We may have a look at what the law of the land of UAE says when someone blocks the road and prays. News from *Gulf News*, published on January 22, 2017:

> "Praying on the side of roads will invite a fine of Dh 1,000".
>
> "Police say such a move is dangerous for road users."
>
> *Abu Dhabi: Motorists who stop their vehicles in undesignated places on the highways to offer prayers will be fined DH 1,000 as the practice poses dangers to them and other road users, Abu Dhabi Police said on Monday."*
> *(GULF NEWS: January 22, 2018)*

On the same day, that same news was published in Jugantar newspaper in Bangladesh;

> "A fine of 23,000 BDT will be levied for leaving vehicles on the road for the praying purpose. The United Arab

> *Emirates has introduced a new rule to bar-stopping cars anywhere on the road. With reference to Abu Dhabi Police Director Lieutenant Colonel Salah Abdullah Al Humairi, Gulf News published the news on Monday." (Jugantar Online Desk January 22, 2018)*

Thank God this news did not come to the notice of our sensitive brothers in Bangladesh. Otherwise, they might have declared Sheikh Khalifa bin Zayed Al Nahyan, the Amir of UAE "Murtad" (apostate for Islam), for hurting religious sentiments. They could have also created mayhem on the streets in the name of religion! Honestly, as the number of religious people in Bangladesh is too large, there should not be any corruption in the country. But it is shameful to recall that after being a five-time world champion in the past with ease, the country is ranked 146th out of 179 countries with 27 points out of 100 in the Corruption Perceptions Index (CPI) published by Transparency International in 2019. And those who have a little less religious sentiments are ranked 21st in the world with 81 points in the same index and 1st place in the Muslim world. Alas, watching the level of corruption does not hurt the feelings of our sensitive countrymen. Allah says in the Holy Qur'an:

كُنْتُمْ خَيْرَ أُمَّةٍ أُخْرِجَتْ لِلنَّاسِ تَأْمُرُونَ بِالْمَعْرُوفِ وَتَنْهَوْنَ عَنِ الْمُنْكَرِ وَتُؤْمِنُونَ بِاللَّهِ ۗ وَلَوْ آمَنَ أَهْلُ الْكِتَابِ لَكَانَ خَيْرًا لَهُمْ ۚ مِنْهُمُ الْمُؤْمِنُونَ وَأَكْثَرُهُمُ الْفَاسِقُونَ (3:110)

"You are now the best people brought forth for humankind. You enjoin what is right and forbid what is wrong and believe in Allah. Had the People of the Book believed it was better for them. Some of them are

believers, but most of them are transgressors." (Surah Al' Imran, verse 110).

And in this regard, the Prophet (peace be upon him) said,

"Whosoever of you sees an evil, let him change it with his hand; and if he is not able to do so, then [let him change it] with his tongue; and if he is not able to do so, then with his heart - and that is the weakest of faith." (Hadith 34, Sahih Muslim)

Rabindranath Tagore also mentioned the same context in his poetry;

"Whoever commits injustice and tolerates injustice, both should be hatred the same way."

If all Bangladeshis considered prayers a religious obligation rather than a social formality to show off and took it as a duty, then there would be no wrongdoing in Bangladesh.

Coming back to the Eid day, I went to perform Eid prayers a little early; I saw no large gathering until then. After a while, I found Hossein and one of his friends in the mosque to offer the Eid prayers. After the prayers, I invited Hossein and his friend to come to my room. I had bought some decorative sweet cookies from the supermarket for Eid. We sat together and ate. Keeping a few sweets for me, I handed the rest to Hossein with a tray and asked him to enjoy Eid with all his friends. After saying goodbye to them, I set off for Sharjah. One thing I noticed on the way was that no animals were being sacrificed in any house.

I have never seen any animal sacrifice in public in Dubai during my last four year's stay. I lived in the apartment then, so I thought there might be no place to sacrifice in the apartments. But now I can see plenty of spaces to offer sacrifice! In Bangladesh, after the prayers, the wind gets chock-a-block with the screams of the sacrificial animals. The yards, roads, and drains become flooded with rivers of the blood of the slaughtered animal. When I went on Hajj in 2013, I did not see any animal sacrifice besides the roads in Saudi Arabia, too, the birthplace of Islam itself. According to the rules of Hajj, a sacrifice was also made in my name. But I did not know where the sacrifice was made. When the Muslim Imam called and told me that my sacrifice had been made, I shaved my head and took a bath. This time, I experienced the same thing in another Arab country. These countries have strict laws on sacrifice or animal slaughter. About this, UAE law says:

> *"Abu Dhabi: It is illegal to slaughter animals in residential premises or public places, and the authorities will be keeping a strict vigil during Eid to prevent such practices, a senior official told Gulf News.*
>
> *If a butcher is caught slaughtering animals illegally, he will be punished as per the labor law. "He may be jailed and deported after the due legal process. His sponsor will be slapped with a Dh 10,000 fine."*

Of course, it is better not to tell our sentimental friends back home about the strict laws of the UAE. Otherwise, it cannot be said with a guarantee that they wouldn't get angry and declare jihad! They might even row across the Bay of Bengal with prehistoric weapons and reach the Persian Gulf. Of course, they are now occupied with solving the Rohingya, Kashmir, and other problems. Although many enthusiastic associates share some true-false pictures on Facebook or other social media in the name of genocide against Muslims in Myanmar, but they do not even know that they are doing more harm than good to the Rohingyas. Once I watched the video of the murder of a Sylheti (Bangladesh) child, Rajan was released in the name of killing Rohingya Muslim children. Seeing that clip, many local brothers and sisters shared the post without verifying the truth. I request, please research a little before sharing anything. In this age of the Information Superhighway, verifying this information is not a difficult task. Lies cannot barricade truth because the power of truth is much more significant, and the truth shall definitely be victorious one day. There are strict instructions in the religious scriptures in this regard. Narrated from Abu Hurairah, the Prophet (peace be upon him) said:

> *"It is enough for a man to prove himself a liar when he goes on narrating whatever he hears." (Muslim) Sahih Muslim 5, Ibn Abi Shaybah 25617, Bukhari. "No liar can ever be a true believer."*

Elvis Presley has said, *"Truth is like the sun. You can shut it out for a time, but it ain't going away."* More than three thousand years ago, the famous Greek philosopher Aristotle said, *"It is dangerous to speak the truth in front of fanatics."* Baul emperor Lalon Fakir said:

"Tell the truth and tread on the right path
Oh, my mind
If you do not know the right trail
You won't achieve the philosophy of life."

Chapter 18

An Unfortunate Bangladeshi Girl

On the day after Eid, I asked Hossein what they did on Eid and where did they go. Hossein replied that after I had left, one of his friends who knew the process of sacrificing animals, took him to a designated slaughterhouse to sacrifice animals for his employer and several others. Curiously, I asked why they did not slaughter the animal by themselves. I don't remember precisely what Hossein replied, but it seems that the people of Arab countries also take the help of Bangladeshi boys to make sacrifices. When I asked what they did with the meat, Hossein uttered that they kept it for themselves. I also have not seen any house or anyone distributing meat from house to house or to the poor. According to the religious law of the people of Bangladesh, sacrificial meat should be divided into three shares. One part should be kept for self, and the other two portions should be distributed among relatives and the poor. In this context, let's have a look at what religion says about this:

> *"A person performing Qurbani may give away all the meat in Sadaqah to the needy. Likewise, a person may keep all the meat for himself. It is not sinful to keep the meat for oneself." Mufti Faraz ibn Adam al-Mahmudi:* <u>www.darulfiqh.com</u>
>
> *Narrated by Aisha, "We used to salt some of the meat of sacrifice and present it to the Prophet at Medina. Once, he said, "Do not eat (of that meat) for more than three days." (Sahih Al Bukhari: Volume 7, Book 68, Number 477)*

In the afternoon, Hossein and his few friends hired a taxi to visit the Cornish area of Abu Dhabi. Hossein's mistress asked him over the phone to take the housemaid with him, so the Bengali housemaid also went with them. Throughout the afternoon, they all roamed the Cornish area together. Cornish is an open space beside Abu Dhabi's Arabian Sea, with a few kilometers of scenic walkways. There is a picturesque panorama of the city's beautiful skyline and tall skyscrapers on the other side. In the evening, they had food at a Bengali restaurant and returned to their places by taxi. This is the joy of Hossein's Eid. Do we ever really think of these Hosseins when we wear new clothes, visit relatives, friends and eat polao-korma, sweets? It seems to me that even Hossein's family does not even know how their beloved husband, son, or father is spending Eid on foreign soil. But for this family's happiness, the Hosseins get peace by sending the entire money home, without thinking of their own well beings.

"Or maybe he's nothing, not incredibly high,
There are miserable wounds and griefs,
Yet all the holy books and the seats of prayer
Are not as holy as the tiny body of a single human."

"Manush" (Human) by Kazi Nazrul Islam

We owe a lot to these Hosseins today. We can never pay them back, but I sincerely pray to the Almighty that we can all lighten the weight of our debts to them, at least a little bit before our last farewell.

I had subscribed to some Bangladeshi TV channels in my room. Sometimes, Hossein and his friend Mr. Taibur Rahman used to come to my room to watch news or dramas especially on the day when the Bangladesh cricket team was playing. Hossein didn't get much time to watch TV, but his friend used to come often. People like us who live abroad cannot separate themselves from Bangladesh's current events and culture. We fall into despair, and our hearts become brimful of sorrow when we hear any news of an accident in the country, like everyone else in Bangladesh. Again, we jump with joy when we see our Tigers (Bangladesh Cricket Team) winning a cricket match. In fact, I am pretty proud that I was born in Bangladesh.

On Thursday, 29th September 2016, I returned from work and went for a walk in the afternoon after taking some rest. That day, Mr. Islam (Bangladeshi driver working next door) had bought a new HTC mobile phone. After returning from the walk, he came to me to seek help in setting up the phone. On the same day, India crossed the Line of Control in Pakistan-administered Azad Kashmir and launched a "surgical strike" against militant pads. Mr. Taibur came to my room with interest and watched the news, maybe because he used to work in BDR (Bangladesh Rifles), which is now known as BGB (Border Guard Bangladesh).

Meanwhile, the presidential election of the United States was approaching as well. He was very concerned about Mr. Trump, so when he asked my opinion, I replied that the Americans would vote for whoever they like. Mr. Taibur's idea was that if Mr. Trump was elected, there would be chaos and danger for Muslims. I tried to persuade him, saying that after the vote, no one in America, like in Bangladesh, would take out even a procession in the streets to protest, nor would they call a strike. They would wait again for the next election. Without that, the whole system cannot be changed in a single election as the President's power is limited. In order to change anything, it has to be passed by the elected two houses. There, the MPs give more priority to the country than the party. Many of them even vote against their party in the parliament. I do not know whether I was able to convince Mr. Taibur with my explanation.

Then unfolded another debate that began with a disagreement. Mr. Taibur expressed his notion that girls in western countries wear short clothes and act unsocially. I told him that if the Western countries' girls feel pleased wearing such dresses, there could be no reason for anyone else to object or form prejudiced opinions. We cannot impose our doctrine on others. Even Western girls can say that in such heat, why do the Arab girls cover their whole body with black cloth. Will that sound acceptable? However, like some programmed software, Mr. Taibur was unwilling to understand; his opinion was since Islam speaks of the veil, so everyone has to follow it. I also said to him, "Westerners have many good virtues and the Arabs also have many barbaric stories to their account. Besides, another friend of yours told me that Hossein was beaten by his master in front of all of you. Is that an example of a civilization?" Mr. Taibur also admitted that he had seen Hossein being beaten. Once, after being beaten, Hossain fled from this master's house. However, later, he was found and brought back.

During the period January 2012 to December 2016 when I was in Dubai, a Pakistani man was in the apartment next to me. On Fridays, he used to ask me to call him when I went to pray. According to him, if the Three-Friday prayers are not offered, the religion will be lost. His younger brother was Hafez of the Quran and worked in Afghanistan. This gentleman did everything unsocial in the eyes of religion, starting with drinking, smoking and whatnot. Almost every night, he would go to the club and bring a girl. Once, he brought a girl who was a Bengali. Later, I saw the girl often came to his room. So, one day, I asked him, "From where do you get so much money for doing all this nonsense?" He said he tricked the girls; he told them he was awaiting his salary and he would give them money once he got his payment. Subsequently, I also noticed that the girl kept coming even without getting any money and spending time with him. I once talked to the girl to find out her story. She was first embarrassed to know that I am also a Bengali, but then she told me about her saddening journey. She was 25 years old; she used to work in a garment factory in Dhaka and make living for her family. She then went to Amman, Jordan through a broker to work for a garment company in Jordan. She worked there for 4/5 years and made a fair amount of money. When she went to Bangladesh on vacation, her sister-in-law's younger sister said to her that she would be able to earn more in Dubai than in Jordan. That relative then lived in Dubai and made all the arrangements for this girl to come to Dubai. Being tempted, the girl came to Dubai rather than going back to Jordan. She landed in Dubai and went to that relative's house where her passport was first seized. Then, after having traveled from Bangladesh to Dubai for the entire day, when she went to bed at night, that woman sent a man into this girl's room and forced her to sleep with him. When she objected, the wicked woman said that she had to spend a lot of money getting a visa and bringing the girl to Dubai, so she had to follow the order. The rest of the story is very much certain.

After staying at that woman's house for six months, she fled from there, but she did not have even a penny. In an unfamiliar place like Dubai, the girl had no other choice. That was why she was doing that independently and had no one to share the money. Back at home, her parents were doing well with the money she sent. I asked her why she spent time with that Pakistani man without money if the purpose is to earn money. I understood from her words that there would be no income during the month of Ramadan; everything is closed during that time. So, the man told her that he would let her stay with him at the time of Ramadan. I heard a strange fact about the Arabs from the girl that many Arabs love to torture girls after having sex. They feel a peculiar thrill in beating them brutally with a belt on the hip. Before Ramadan came, I heard that the girl became pregnant, and the Pakistani man chased her away. He also changed the SIM card of his phone. After that, I never saw the girl in that apartment again. But since the Pakistani often went to the club, they met again. The girl was married to an Indian man by then (this is why I have hidden the girl's name and identity). Meanwhile, a Filipino girl replaced the Bengali girl in the house of that Pakistani man.

~~~

"That girl who swaps from one to another every night,
Life goes on with her curse.
Protesting against all odds is part of life,
Stopping after reaching the goal,
Trading dream is life,
Fighting back when there's nowhere to go,
Coming home every day, complex calculations running in mind,
Saying "I don't want this life" is life after all."

Artist: Nachiketa
Music Director: Nachiketa

~~~

After some time, I heard the story of the disgrace of another Bengali woman and her underage daughter in the hands of the same Pakistani man. That was in Maryland in the United States, but for now, let's come back to the Middle East.

I often heard from my friends in Dubai that they used to raise money and arrange for one or another oppressed Bangladeshi to take shelter, get a new passport through the Bangladesh embassy, buy a plane ticket and send him/her home. The local police's cooperation is very much needed in this regard, as a police report is essential to get a new passport. However, gathering the documents was a dangerous job; if the concerned person got caught, he/she would be sent back to the old employer. Without the permission of the previous boss, it is almost impossible to leave the country.

"Life is a path without end
Life is just talking about life
Life goes on
Life is just a game of addition and subtraction

Life is the tomb of dreams
In the secret room of the mind, the beast lives
Cherishing life is life."

Artist: Nachiketa
Music Director: Nachiketa

Chapter 19

My Departure

On the 1st of October 2016, Mr. Taibur Rahman came to watch the Bangladesh-Afghanistan cricket match, we watched the game together, and Bangladesh won the series on that day. We both had a lot of fun. We also watched the Bangladesh-England cricket match on the 7th of October. Bangladesh opener Imrul Kayes scored 112 runs, but the rest of the team could not score 35 runs with six wickets in hand. Even in the game on the 12th of October, Bangladesh lost to England after scoring 278 runs. Mr. Taibur came that day to watch the game. Although he was interested in watching cricket, Hossein couldn't manage time to enjoy any match. The cricket match lasts for 6/7 hours; it is too much time for Hossein. If the call comes from inside the house and he doesn't show up on time, the consequence will be devastating. So, he used to come from time to time and went back to work again after watching for a while. Hossein works as long as he stays awake.

There were some trainees of the police training college in a villa in that area. After training all week, they spend the Fridays and Saturdays elsewhere. There was a boy named Rahman who used to cook for them. His house is in Sandip, Bangladesh. The weekends were pretty much relaxed for him since no one was there in the villa. His condition was a little better than others; he was earning a bit more money. When he saw me walking around in the afternoon, he thought I also worked in a house there. I used to talk to him in the same way. One day, through Hossein, Rahman got to know me, upon learning, he felt really ashamed and started apologizing.

I tried to convince him that he had done nothing to be ashamed of and apologize. I am a very ordinary person, just like them. By the grace of God, I have an American seal on my passport today, and they don't have it. This is the difference. He told me that he had saved some money and in few days, he was going to the country on vacation to get married. Two days later, in the evening, I saw Hossein and some of his friends were taking him to the airport via taxi to see off; I wished him for his marriage.

In most places, the Arabs live in the same area with their various relatives of the same tribe. I heard from Hossein which of the houses nearby was his owner's brother's house, the owner's sister's house, which was his cousin's house. The house next to Hossein's owner's home was his brother's house. After Eid, on the 14th of October, the brother's daughter's wedding ceremony was scheduled. The whole place, even the outer boundary wall, was lit up a week before the main event.

Here, no outsider is invited to the wedding, only confined to close relatives. The program lasted for a week. On the day of the main ceremony, music is played until late at night. So, during that time, Hossein's workload also increased. He had to make afternoon snacks, dinner and handle a lot of other things. Besides, the owner came with his youngest wife to the empty house of his sister next door. The owner wanted to build another building next to the main building. So, Hossein also has to provide food for the master and the third wife.

I once asked Hossein if he had ever talked about increasing his salary. Hossein answered with a smile, "I fear that I will lose everything, be beaten and chased away if I talk about raising my wage. I will be in deep trouble then. I just want to be satisfied with what I get." From time to time, I heard Mr. Islam from Chittagong (Bangladeshi driver next door) advised Hossein to accompany him to speak to Hossein's owner; if the owner fired Hossein, the driver would tell his owner to arrange a job at his house. Although Hossein did not have a school or college education, he understood that many could only instigate, but nobody actually helps.

Moreover, Hossein knew that new visas for Bangladeshis were closed in the UAE for several years. Once the visa is canceled, there will be nothing left to do; he will have to leave the country with a burden. I asked Hossein if Mr. Islam can arrange another job for him? Hossein said in reply that Mr. Islam himself was always afraid that at some point, he would lose his job. That was why he went on vacation, got married, and came back early. So, I gave only one piece of advice to Hossein in this regard, "Hossein, you will understand your well-being, do whatever you think is right." Suddenly, I decided to return to the United States in the first week of

November with special needs. I also informed Hossein about that in time.

Immediately Hossein's mind was filled with oceanic desolation. Hossein had high hopes, and he also requested me several times to show him as a brother in the papers and take him to the United States. I tried to convince Hossein that it was not possible because all my brothers and sisters, and relatives are given to the US Immigration Office. I told him that if it was possible to arrange his immigration through legal channels, I would definitely try it. But he still tried to change my mind.

One day, he called his mother and asked her to talk to me. The lady prayed for me and asked me to stay for a few more days. I became a bit saddened upon hearing the plea. I told her that I might have to come again. But I had to go back that time. I must go where the job takes me. But I would always remember Hossein.

When I broke the news to my native brothers at work that I was leaving, they too became speechless. I gave them a bit of advice to at least prioritize the mother tongue in the job. I may not stay forever, but someone else will come in my place, and he will look after their interest. During my four years of service, we were able to increase the number of Bangladeshi workers from few to 185 out of more than half a thousand local workers. The second-largest number of workers was 155 Indians, 65 Pakistanis, and the rest were Nepalese, Sri Lankans, Filipinos, and a few Africans. But the unfortunate thing is that the foreign love of the people of Bangladesh is well known. Although Bengali is one of the world's most spoken six languages in terms of numbers, yet Bangladeshi love to speak in foreign languages whenever they get a chance. In the Middle

East, I have seen that average workers forget their mother tongue and switch to Urdu or Hindi. Although they have not been able to speak monochromatic Arabic for 10/15 years, but they love to speak fluent Urdu. Most Bangladeshi people have limited Arabic knowledge, mostly, their vocabulary is limited to 'Insha'Allah', 'Masha 'Allah', 'Alhamdulillah', 'Subhan 'Allah', etc. Looking up at a little higher level, the situation remains the same, only the practice of English is a little more persistent. Arabic culture and the Urdu language have been absorbed very quickly.

When I arrived on this land, I was confused by the local Bangladeshi at that moment. What is the need for mother-tongue if they know Hindi/Urdu? They did not or do not have the idea to realize the far-reaching consequences of this. As a result, none of those who came to replace me have understood the condition of the workers in the last four years. And that is why the number of Bangladeshi workers has come down from 185 to almost zero. Instead, Indian, Nepali, Sri Lankan, and Filipino workers are ruling. Precisely, the same situation prevails in my current job. In the last four years, from a small number, now there are about three hundred and fifty Bangladeshi workers. The day I will not be here, workers from other countries may dominate. I have no animosity or discrimination towards people of any other country. It is my wish that all people of all countries should be able to keep their heads high with dignity. Unfortunately, not many well-known people or institutions, including their lands' embassies, take care of them. The number of individuals or organizations looking after the interests of Bangladeshis is very few. Being caught in brokers' clutches in the country, they go abroad searching for the wild goose, but they find every way is blocked after coming here.

Gradually the day of my return drew closer. As soon as I informed Hossein that I was leaving, I saw the face of the always smiling Hossein turning into a web of wrinkles. It seemed that happiness was something light years away from him. Slowly I started packing things in between work and off-days. I gave all my old clothes and rarely used stuff to Hossein one by one. When giving the things, Hossein used to say, "I will take these later after you leave." Maybe, he was still hoping if I would change my mind. On the final day, Hossein came several times in the middle of work and talked. My flight was at 10 pm, so I stayed in the room until the evening. One by one, my colleagues came and bid goodbye. One of my colleagues, Bill, gave me a ride to the airport in his car. Before I departed, Hossein came in the evening and put my bags in the car.

"The carriage is ready; it's afternoon;
The late autumnal sun blazes;
A midday breeze swirls dust
Off the deserted rural road;
In the cool shade of a peepal tree

What immense sadness has engulfed
The entire sky and the whole world!
The farther I go, the more clearly I hear
Those poignant words "Won't let you go!"
From world's end to the blue dome of the sky
Echoes the eternal cry: "Won't let you go!"
Everything cries, "I won't let you go!

> *And yet, alas, we have to let go; and however,*
> *Of course, we must go. And this is how it has been,*
> *From time immemorial."*
>
> — *"Sonar Tori" by Rabindranath Tagore*

~~~

After saying goodbye to Hossein for the last time, we left for the airport. Gradually, Bill's car crossed the parking lot and steered towards the main road. I looked back several times before the car navigated to the big highway and saw Hossein standing alone under the lamp post in front of my former villa that I had just left. Though the car had accelerated to a distance, but I could very well imagine the think film of tears in Hossein's eyes. I don't know if he had low hopes like Ratan from the short story "Postmaster" written by Tagore;

> *"But Ratan had no philosophy. She was wandering about the post office in a flood of tears. It may be that she had still a lurking hope in some corner of her heart that her Dada would return, and that is why she could not tear herself away. Alas for our foolish human nature! Its fond mistakes are persistent. The dictates of reason take a long time to assert their own sway. The surest proofs, meanwhile, are disbelieved. False hope is clung to with all one's might and main, till a day comes when it has sucked the heart dry, and it forcibly breaks through its bonds and departs. After that comes the misery of awakening, and then once again the longing to get back into the maze of the same mistakes."*
>
> —*The Postmaster (1918), translated by Debendranath Mitra, published in 'Stories from Tagore'*

"O' I stopped for few days on the way
I had worn the garland of love around my neck
My accolade-garland is going to be torn
I will not stay with you any longer
Dayal (God) has called me."

-Artist: Andrew Kishor

Hossein

I left the UAE in November 2016 and stayed in the USA till May 2017. Then I came back to this region, Qatar, for another assignment. Since then, I have been living here to find more tragic life stories like Hossein. Like the ones shared in this book, some chronicles could be a little less spine-chilling, yet soul-stirring and tear-jerking narratives still take the lead.

Chapter 20

Qatar

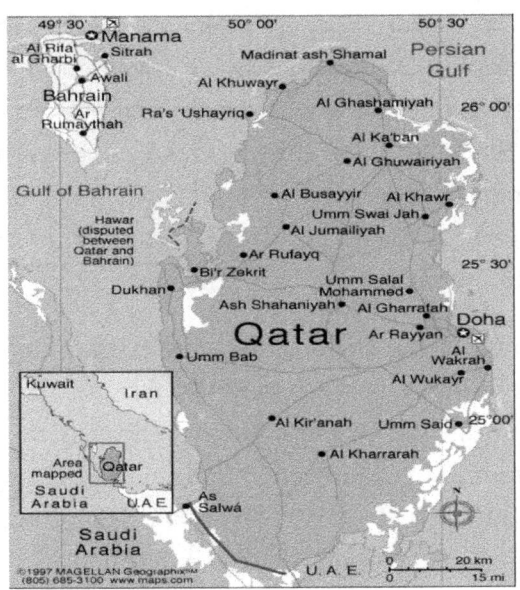

Qatar is a tiny nation in Arabian Peninsula located amid the Arabian Gulf's western coast. It shares its southern border with Saudi Arabia and a maritime border between Bahrain, the United Arab Emirates, and Iran. Its total land surface measures 11,437 square kilometers (about 4415.85 Square miles). Qatar's coastline along the Persian Gulf is 563 kilometers (about 350 miles) long covers three sides of the country. The land border with Saudi Arabia in the south is 60 kilometers (37 miles) long, and United Arab Emirates (UAE). Qatar's northwest coast is fewer than thirty kilometers (18.5 miles) from Bahrain. Doha is the capital of the country and the central administrative, commercial, and population center. The vast majority of the population (about 92%) live in Doha, the capital.

In 1971, Qatar and Bahrain were proposed to join and become part of the United Arab Emirates. But both Qatar and Bahrain decided against the merger and instead, formed independent nations. Qatar declared independence on September 3, 1971. Since its complete independence from Britain in 1971, Qatar has emerged as one of the world's most important oil and gas producers. Since 2013, the country has been governed by HH Sheikh Tamim bin Hamad bin Khalifa Al-Thani. Sheikh Jassim bin Mohammed Al Thani (Arabic: جاسم بن محمد آل ثاني; c. 1825 – July 17, 1913), was the founder of the State of Qatar.

Though Arabic is the official language of Qatar, English is well-spoken and understood nationwide. English is considered the second language in the country. The climate is hot and extremely humid in the summer. Summer temperatures range average of 30° C (86⁰ F) to 50° C (122⁰ F). The official currency is the Qatari Riyal (average 3.65 QR = 1 USD).

It is an Islamic State whose laws and customs follow the Islamic tradition. The Qataris are mainly Sunni Muslims. Islam is the official religion, and Islamic jurisprudence is the basis of Qatar›s legal system. A significant minority of the population is Hindu. Qataris constitute only 10% of the country's total population, and Qataris are considered a 'minority' in their own nation. The remaining 90% is made up of a workforce of over a hundred different nationalities.

List of Nationalities and Their Population

Nationality	Population	Total Percentile
India	700,000	21.8%
Bangladesh	400,000	12.5%
Nepal	400,000	12.5%
Qatar	333,000	9.35%
Egypt	300.000	9.35%
Philippines	236,000	7.35%
Pakistan	150,000	4.7%
Sri Lanka	140,000	4.35%
Sudan	60,000	1.9%
Syria	54,000	1.7%
Jordan	51,000	1.6%
Lebanon	40,000	1.25%
USA	40,000	1.25%
Kenya	30,000	1%
Iran	30,000	1%
Indonesia	27,350	0.85%
Tunisia	26,000	0.8%
Ethiopia	25,000	0.8%
UK	22,000	0.7%
Nigeria	11,000	0.35%
China	More than 10,000	0.3%
Turkey	10,000	0.3%
Canada	9,200	0.3%
Saudi Arabia	8,245	0.25%

Source: onlineqatar.com

References:

https://www.worldometers.info/world-population/qatar-population/
http://priyadsouza.com/population-of-qatar-by-nationality-in-2017
https://www.britannica.com/
https://www.infoplease.com/world/countries/qatar
https://www.mofa.gov.qa/

Chapter 21

Job in the Middle East: All You Need to Know

First, find a government-approved trusted broker if you cannot do everything yourself. One of the essential things for workers to know before coming to the Middle East is that most companies bear the cost of hiring. This includes visas and airfare. A substantial share of the millions you spend goes into the broker's pocket. So, you should not give one more penny than the required sanctioned fees by the government. We have already learned from Mr. Razzak in Dubai or Mr. Mojibar in Qatar, Sarbindu, and Anshuman in India that the company hires people and bears all costs if it needs them. Under any circumstances, no cash should be given to the broker. You need to pay by check or money order — that way, a legal document is established for any future reference. If someone demands more money than the government allows, then there must be something wrong. Therefore, people need to be alerted when the brokers demand more cash. It would help if you are more careful to find all necessary information yourself or through a very trusted person. If the research work is not done gingerly, in most cases, the results are not favorable.

Find out the details of where you will work for the company before giving money to someone. You should not leave the country without a written appointment letter, including how many hours you have to work daily, salary, overtime pay, weekly day-offs, pay if you are sick, annual or biennial leave, etc. Employers give 30 to 40 days off every two years and also pay for the round-trip airfare. So, seek clarification of your employer's position on this. If possible, consult a lawyer of any non-profit organization before signing any document. No matter which agreement you sign, you will keep 2/3 copies of it with your family members back in Bangladesh and always keep one copy with you. With this agreement, you, the Bangladesh Embassy, or the Labor Department abroad will be able to provide legal assistance against the company on your behalf. An oral contract without a written one is not acceptable in any court. In many cases, despite knowing a lot, we could not help many people because there is no written agreement.

It is must-needed to know the company's name, address, phone number and find further information about the company by yourself or with someone close to you and keep your future clear. If possible, get information by contacting the embassy of the concerned country. It should be remembered that caution is a must. You are the one who can make your life beautiful or miserable. It would be best if you do not come abroad by selling houses, deposits, or borrowing money at interest. If you have to borrow money, you should borrow a small amount from a conventional bank. Borrow as much you can afford to pay back easily. If you have to go back to Bangladesh like Nayan, Zakir, Akhtar, or Mallik, at least you can pay the debt by working there. You don't have to stay after being tortured here abroad.

Labor rights are well protected under UAE law, and it is vital to know about your legal rights. Here are ten facts that you need to know about working in the UAE:

1. *You have a right to annual leave.*
   All workers should take leave on public holidays.

2. *You should always get paid regularly.*
   Workers employed in return for an annual or a monthly wage have to be paid at least once per month.

3. *Your employer cannot deny you maternity leave.*
   The UAE Labour Law, Federal Law No. 8, Article No. 30, states as follows: "A female worker shall be entitled to maternity leave with full pay for 45 days.

4. *Your employer is not allowed to keep your passport.*
   An employer cannot ask you to hand over your passport to keep in their custody without your written consent.

5. *You should never bear the costs of your residency visa.*
   According to the UAE labor law, visa expenses must be borne by the employer. You, as an employee, are never required to reimburse your employer for visa costs at any time. Visa costs and sponsorship costs are the sole responsibility of the employer.

6. *You should work no more than 8 or 9 hours a day.*
   The maximum number of ordinary working hours for adult workers shall be eight hours per day or forty-eight hours per week. The usual working hours shall be reduced by two hours during Ramadan. The worker's commutation periods from residence to the worksite shall not be calculated within the working hours.

7. *Want to resign? You do not need your employer's consent.*
   The Labor Law does not require the consent of the employer for resigning from a job. This is your own decision to make. You cannot be forced to quit either.

8. *If you leave, you need to complete your notice period.*
   Your notice period is mandatory. You have to keep in mind that the notice period mentioned in the contract is compulsory for all labor contracts as agreed upon between the employer and employee. It is usually no less than 30 days.

9. *When you resign, you are entitled to gratuity.*
   Gratuity pay is calculated based on the most recent salary paid into your account without allowances and bonuses. It can be different depending on whether your contract was limited or unlimited.

10. *You have the right to a grace period after your work visa is terminated.*
    After termination of employment contract and cancellation of work visa, the terminated employee is granted a 30-day grace period from the cancellation date. He can either obtain a new residence permit or leave the country.

-Source Gulf News

In this regard, the law of the Department of Labor of Qatar states:

1. ***Ensure complete understanding of your employment contract.*** *Employment contracts are drawn up in bilingual form; thoroughly read the one you can understand (or can easily and completely be translated to you) and see to it that the following items are clearly stated in the contract:*
   - *Employer name, place of work, and type of work*
   - *Proof of identification including full name, exact qualifications, nationality, residence, and profession*
   - *Term start and end dates of contract (contract period)*
   - *Agreed salary rate, salary disbursement, and salary release schedule*

2. ***Your employer assumes responsibility for your visa expenses.*** *Ensure this clause is present in the contract. You may also request an additional clause to allow you to switch sponsors later if you wish, but know that this is not a guaranteed addition to the contract.*

Under no circumstances should you lose your passport by stepping on foreign soil. In some countries, it is illegal for an employer to keep an employee's passport. Qatari law says;

> *"Confiscation of Passports: Under no circumstances can an employer hold a worker's passport. However, since the law typically holds sponsors liable for the debts and obligations of their workers, some sponsors can retain the passports of their employees until these matters are resolved."*

Many companies withhold salaries from employees for two to three months. That too is illegal;

Law No. 1 of 2015 – Wage Protection System:

> "The law orders that employers pay the salaries of their employees through direct bank transfers made from the employer's local Qatari account, in Qatari currency, to a Qatari account in the name of the employee. The new system intends to address previous problems of late or missing payments by requiring companies to register their employee's details with the state's banking regulator, Qatar Central Bank, and pay employees at least once per month."

Register your name at the nearest Bangladesh Embassy. Simultaneously, there are non-profit and non-political events called Bangladesh Forum (or other names) in different countries; it will help keep in touch with them. Women shouldn't come with the job as a housemaid. However, there is no difficulty in opting for different professions including teaching, nursing or other medical subjects, sales associate, and customer service. In this case, you need to know some Arabic and English.

I have shared the information that I have learned from the experience of the last eight years; if this information benefits even one person, then I would think my efforts have borne fruit.

Chapter 22

Seven Deadly Sins

"Sin creates [an inclination to] Sin; it engenders vice by repetition of the same acts. This results in perverse inclinations that cloud conscience and corrupt the concrete judgment of good and evil. Thus Sin tends to reproduce itself and reinforce itself, but it cannot destroy the moral sense at its root." (Para. 1865, <u>Catechism of the Catholic Church</u>, 1994)

Seven deadly sins prescribed by Mohandas Karamchand Gandhi, a great leader, and creator of India's nonviolent movement, are among the most influential figures in modern social and political activism. These traits are considered to be most spiritually dangerous to humanity. The Seven Deadly Sins are the transgressions that are fatal to spiritual progress. People probably commit some of them every day without thinking about the horrible tradition of eternal damnation in which they are participating. In 1947, a year before his assassination, Mahatma Gandhi gave his grandson, Arun Gandhi, a paper piece. On that piece of paper, Gandhi had written what he called the seven blunders of the world.

- *Wealth without Work*
- *Pleasure without Conscience*
- *Knowledge without Character*
- *Science without Humanity*
- *Commerce without Morality*
- *Politics without Principle*
- *Worship without Sacrifice*

1. **Wealth without work**

Wealth has replaced work as the foundational value in our country. We want to be wealthy rather than get wealthy. There is nothing wrong with wealth, but there is something crucial about work deeds. Work is central to human nature. Work builds character. We need to work, be productive, be useful, and add value to life through our work. Wealth should not be the goal of work but a by-product of working well. The world is filled with financial advice on how to get rich with a modest investment. The ones that aren't complete scams usually involve investing in the stock market. The purveyors of financial products tout the high yields that the stock market consistently offers.

Gandhi often rallied against the world's materialism and mourned over the growing gap between those who do an honest day's work and the ones who sit back and profit from another's work. Gandhi once said there are enough resources in the world for everyone's need, but not for everyone's greed.

Wealth without work is temporary. It cannot and will not last forever.

2. **Pleasure without conscience**

We often justify our actions by the good feelings they bring us rather than by the amount of good they do. Conscience is the gauge that tells us how well our efforts approximate our ethical ideals. Conscience rooted in the shared suffering of life and the interdependence of all things help us shape our choices and actions that flow from them in the service of others and ourselves.

The ultimate costs of pleasures without conscience are high, measured in time, money, reputation, and wounding. The hearts and minds of other people, who are adversely affected by those who want to indulge, gratify themselves in a short time. It's dangerous to pull or lull away from natural law without conscience. Conscience is essentially the repository of timeless truths and principles - the internal monitor of natural law.

Arun Gandhi, writing about his grandfather's "seven blunders of the world", says that pleasure without conscience connects to wealth without work. He says, *"People find imaginative and dangerous ways of bringing excitement to their otherwise dull lives. Their search for pleasure and excitement often ends up costing society very heavily."* Gandhi believed pleasure must come from within the soul and excitement from serving the needy, caring for the family, the children, and relatives. Building sound human relationships can be an exciting and adventurous activity. Unfortunately, we ignore life's spiritual pleasures and indulge in physical pleasures, which are 'pleasure without conscience'.

(A Sermon by Jim Ketcham. Based on II Samuel 11:1 --12:7a. First Preached at University Baptist Church)

3. **Knowledge without character**

Little knowledge is dangerous but even more dangerous is much knowledge without a strong, principled character. Knowledge is power and the currency of power, but knowledge itself is value-neutral. Unless we value such core decencies as honesty, compassion, justice, and self-reliance; all the knowledge in the world won't save us from ourselves.

The knowledge argument aims to establish that conscious experience involves non-physical properties. It rests on the idea that someone who has complete physical knowledge about another conscious being might lack knowledge about how it feels to have that being's experiences. It is one of the most discussed arguments against physicalism. Our obsession with materialism tends to make us more concerned about acquiring knowledge to get a better job and make more money. A lucrative career demands an illustrious character. Our educational centers emphasize career-building and not character-building. Gandhi believed if one cannot understand oneself, how can one know the philosophy of life. He used to tell the story of a young man who was an outstanding student throughout his academic career, scored "A's" in every subject, and strove harder and harder to maintain his grades. The young man became a bookworm. However, when he passed with distinction and got a lucrative job, he could not deal with people, nor could he build relationships. Besides, now he had no time to learn these essential aspects of life.

Consequently, he could not live with his wife and children nor work with his colleagues. His life ended up being miserable.

All those years of study and excellent grades did not bring him happiness. Therefore, it is not true that a person who is successful in amassing wealth is necessarily happy. An education that ignores character-building is incomplete.

4. Commerce (business) without morality (ethics)

There should be no human endeavor free of conscience and moral consequence. We have to reclaim the importance of honest livelihood, insisting that earning a living should not be at the expense of others or our higher selves. We must reclaim the link between business and holiness. As in wealth without work, we indulge in commerce without morality to make more money by any means possible. Price gouging, palming off inferior products, cheating, and making false claims are a few of the obvious ways in which we indulge in commerce without morality. There are also thousands of other ways in which we do immoral or unethical business. When profit-making becomes an essential aspect of business, morals, and ethics usually go overboard. Suppose business leaders ignore the moral foundation and allow economic systems to operate without a moral foundation and continued education. In this case, they will soon create an amoral, if not immoral, society and business. Economic and political systems are ultimately based on a moral foundation. Every business transaction is a moral challenge to see that both parties come out legally.

How moralists evaluate business depends upon the fundamental moral principles. Most moral philosophies have included the assumption that morality and practicality are two different things. Older moralists typically argued that morality's demands conflicted with business practicality requirements and so condemned business. More recent moralists tend to adopt a less extreme version of the dichotomy, holding that determining practical and moral values involves following two distinct thought lines. Gandhi encouraged everyone to spin their own cloth and make their own clothing. One of Gandhi's followers' soul force vows was wearing and creating homespun clothing. It gave them a sense of self-sufficiency and a sense of cleanliness. They could not participate in commerce without morality and still be the ones committed to nonviolence.

5. Science without Humanity

Just because we can do something doesn't mean we ought to do it. Science need not be in the service of humanity — there is an important place for pure research — but science ought not to be at the expense of humanity. We need to understand what they are working on and the implications of that work on humankind. We need to know where science may be taking us and decide if we want to go there. If science becomes all technique and technology, it quickly degenerates into man against humanity. Technologies come from the paradigms of science. And if there's very little understanding of the higher human purposes that the technology is striving to serve, we become victims of our own technocracy. We see otherwise highly educated people climbing the scientific ladder of success, even though it's often missing the rung called humanity and leaning against the wrong wall.

The majority of the scientists who ever lived or live today have brought about a scientific and technological explosion in the world to advance human lives. But if all they do is superimpose technology on the same old problems, not fundamental changes, we may see an evolution, an occasional "revolution" in science. Without humanity, we see precious little real human advancement. All the old inequities and injustices are still with us.

A world created by science can be run safely only by the science's spirit and methods that made it and started science. It is impossible to create a new world through science and then run it based on outdated, sentimental principles like fear, lust for power, and domination. Science has two central values to offer, which can help build a new world. The one is its spirit, and the other its method. *(Science Week, 2002. Retrieve on March 14 from www.scienceweek.com)*

6. Religion without Sacrifice

One person's faith is another person's fantasy because religion has reduced to meaningless rituals practiced mindlessly. Temples, churches, synagogues, mosques, and those entrusted with the duty of interpreting religion to laypeople seek to control through fear of hell, damnation, and purgatory. In the name of God, they have spawned more hate and violence than any government. True religion is based on spirituality, love, compassion, understanding, and appreciation of each other, whatever our beliefs may be -- Christians, Jews, Hindus, Muslims, Buddhists, Atheists, Agnostics, or whatever. Gandhi believed whatever labels we put on our faith, ultimately, all of us worship Truth because Truth is God. Superficially we may be very devout believers and make an outstanding public show of our worship. Still, if that belief, understanding, compassion, love, and appreciation does not translate into our lives, prayers will have no meaning. Genuine worship demands sacrifice, not just in terms of the number of times we say our blessings but also how sincere we are in translating those prayers into lifestyles.

Without sacrifice, human beings may become active in a church but remain inactive in their gospel. In other words, they may go for the social facade of religion and the righteousness of religious practices. There is no real walking with people or going the second mile, or dealing with their social problems that may eventually undo the economic system. It takes sacrifice to serve other people's needs - the gift of their pride and prejudice, among other things. If a church or religion is another hierarchical system, its members won't have a sense of service or inner worship. Instead, they will be into outward observances and all the visible accouterments of religion. But they are neither God-centered nor principle-centered. Authentic faith is not about getting into heaven; it is about helping your neighbor here in hell. God doesn't want your praise; God wants your deeds: so do justly, love mercy, walk humbly. *"If religion doesn't help you put others first, it isn't worthy of your time, your money, your respect, or your loyalty." (Sunday, February 26, 2006. Rabbi Rami Shapiro. Sojourner's magazine, a liberal Christian publication edited by Jim Wallis)*

7. Politics without Principles

Contemporary politics is about power and privilege, not principle. People everywhere want to help create a better world – people are deeply concerned about widespread suffering, environmental destruction, escalating materialism, and losing the sense of community. There is a deep and growing hunger for a wiser and more loving society. Gandhi and Dr. King modeled the vision to create such a culture. The principles I think Gandhi was talking about were the principles that helped most people. The direction that we are all created in God's image is the principle that all people have a right to dignity, a home, food, healthcare, and freedom. Any politics that denies one of these tenets is unprincipled politics.

Gandhi said those who firmly believe in nonviolence should never stand for elections, but they should elect representatives willing to understand and practice the philosophy. Gandhi said an elected representative is the one on whom we have bestowed our power of attorney. Such a person should be allowed to wield authority only as long as s/he enjoys our confidence. When politicians indulge in power games, they act without principles. However, to remain in power at all costs is unethical. Gandhi said when politicians (or anyone else, for that matter) give up the pursuit of Truth, it will doom them in the case of parties. Partisan politics, lobbying, bribing, and other forms of malpractice that are so rampant in politics today is also dishonesty. Politics has earned the reputation of being dirty. It is so because we made it corrupt. We create power groups to lobby for our cause and are willing to do anything to achieve our goal. *(M.K. Gandhi Institute 1998-2005.* http://www.gandhiinstitute.org/Library*)*

Justice and judgment are inevitably inseparable, suggesting that to the degree people move away from the laws of nature, the decision will be adversely affected. People get distorted notions. They start telling rational lies to explain why things work or why they don't. They move away from the law of "the farm" into social/political environments. The people who are transforming education today are doing it by building consensus around a standard set of principles, values, and priorities and debunking the high degree of specialization, departmentalization, and partisan politics. If there is no principle, there is no real norm, nothing you can depend on. The focus on the personality ethic is the instant creation of an image that sells well in the social and economic marketplace. Politicians spend millions of dollars to create an image, even though it's superficial and lacks substance, but they rain money bills to get votes and gain office.

To some, these principles and the ideals they represent are readily attributable to the leaders of distinction, such as Mahatma Gandhi. Still, such notable leaders are harder to find in the much more common experiences of everyday living. In response to this concern, Gandhi replied, *"I claim to be no more than an average man with less than average ability. I am not a visionary. I claim to be a practical idealist. Nor can I claim any special merit for what I have been able to achieve with laborious research. I have not the shadow of a doubt that any man or woman can achieve what I have if he or she would make the same effort and cultivate the same hope and faith."*

Bibliography.

Para. 1865, <u>Catechism of the Catholic Church</u>, *1994*
A Sermon by Jim Ketcham. Based on II Samuel 11:1 --12:7a. First Preached at University Baptist Church
Science Week, 2002. Retrieve on March 14 from www.scienceweek. com
Sunday, February 26, 2006. Rabbi Rami Shapiro. Sojourner's magazine, a liberal Christian publication edited by Jim Wallis
M.K. Gandhi Institute 1998-2005. <u>http://www.gandhiinstitute.org/Library</u>
Ciulla, Joanne B., Ph.D. The Ethics of Leadership. 2003. Wadsworth/Thomson Learning Belmont. CA. 94002-3098.
Covey, Stephen. Principle-Centered Leadership. 1990. Free Press. New York, NY. 10020.

Chapter 23

My Motivational Speech

6 D's: The 6 Important Building Blocks
Focus on D's and walk the miles of success

From the lens of my experience and learnings, I have hatched a rulebook of 6 D's that I follow holistically, which have fetched me remarkable results. Not only this, but I have also shared these D's with my friends and associates, and even they have sparked off reward-reaping results after applying these in their lives.

1. The first "D" starts with a "**Dream**". A journey begins with a dream. It should be the dream we envision when we are awake, not when we are sleeping. What we see at night is the hallucination dream. On August 28, 1963, at the Lincoln Memorial in Washington DC, Dr. Martin Luther King, Jr. delivered his iconic speech, "I have Dream". Though Dr. King did not live through to see his dream come true, but the vision that he implemented to our great nation

materialized long after his death. So, we can dream about ourselves, our families, our communities, or the country. Remember, all of us owe to our family, our country and humanity. So, if we bring our dream to fruition, it means we are giving something back to our family, our country and mankind. Every individual's success means the success of the country.

2. The second "D" is choosing a "**Destination**". We must harbor a dream about a destination. A journey without a target destination means sailing on a rudderless ship, where we are at the mercy of the waves. Therefore, we usually end up reaching where we do not want to. Remember, the outcome you expect is usually what you expect. If you are heading to a no-destination zone, any road can take you there. I have seen students completing more than two hundred credit hours but have not received a degree yet, even though most colleges require only 125 to 130 credit hours to complete a bachelor's degree. When you choose a destination, always select like the Air Force slogan says, "Aim High". It would be best if you always aim high. If you aim at achieving 100%, you may or may not get 100%, but you will reach very close. But if you desire 70%, I am almost certain that you will never achieve above 70%. So why shortchange yourself. My late father gave me one of the best pieces of advice in my life. After I graduated from High School, I informed him that I wanted to be a scientist, and for that reason, I wanted to study Applied Physics & Electronics. My father said to me, "Son, choice of life, and choice of a wife are the most crucial decisions in your life. If you make any mistake in making either one of these decisions, you will suffer for the rest of your life.

It's you who shall have to decide whether you want to be a doctor, engineer, scientist, or businessman. Your future life will depend on the decision that you are making now. A similar thing will happen when you decide to marry someone."

3. The third "D" in the list is "**Determination**". You may have a Dream and a target Destination but may not have Determination; no Determination is as good as you have no dream or destination. Therefore, ensure that you are determined to reach your destination. Life is full of surprises; it may not be an easy path to reach your goal. Let me share my life story about how I was determined to achieve my dreamed destination. Born in Kushtia, Bangladesh, challenge befriended me in the very early years. It was a historic time in the short history of gaining independence. Amidst the ripple effects of independence warfare, my primary and secondary education began in Kushtia. Upon completing my secondary education in 1980, I left Kushtia and studied Applied Physics & Electronics at Dhaka University. Scientists like Professor Bose, who is known for Bose-Einstein Condensate, was a physics professor at Dhaka University. In March 1982, in my pursuit of higher education with no outside support and the challenge of living abroad, I boarded an aircraft to continue my higher educational journey in the United States of America. On March 17, 1982, I came to the US with $1300.00 in my pocket. I was only 19 years old at that time. After paying the first-semester tuition fee and apartment rent, I only had $125.00 left for food and other expenses. And this happened not just in the first month. For a long time, I had to live on a shoestring budget. Although I had

a destination and I was determined, yet my journey to my destination was not like a plain sail. There were times I lived a homeless life, living in a Mosque or friend's couch, ate only on times when people gave me something to eat. But I did not let the wick of my determination fade away, and, at age 33, from homeless, I became a corporate owner. I established my own corporation. At some point, more or less than 50 employees depended on the paycheck that I signed. I also did not receive my first bachelor's degree until I was 45, then my master's degree at age 47. One thing that kept me going; I was "Determined" to reach my "Destination".

4. Fourth "D" is "**Devotion or Dedication**". Make sure that you dedicate your time and efforts to reach your destination. Take one step at a time. Do not jump over. If you are not determined and devoted, you may not be able to fulfill the goal of your life. As I said earlier, life is full of surprises. You may have to cross a lot of bumpy roads. However, always stay focused and devote your time and energy to reach your dreamed destination.

5. The fifth "D" that I follow is "**Discipline**". We may foster a myth in our lives that discipline is only for Uniformed Service Personnel. That is wrong, my friends. Everybody should have discipline in his or her life. If you are determined to maintain discipline and dedicate a part of your time towards your destination, you will certainly reach there one day. Remember: "Drops of water make an ocean, and grains of sand make a continent." So, little drops of effort every day will give you massive success in the end. I know it's tough to take the first step but little

strokes fell great oaks. So, once you take that first step and keep going, the rest would be easy.

6. The sixth and final "D" is "**Do not Derail** from your Destination". The 11th President A.P.J. Abdul Kalam (2002 to 2007) of India (the World's most populous democratic country) said, "'FAIL' stands for **F**irst **A**ttempt **I**n **L**earning. Failure is not the opposite of success. It is a part of success." If you are not successful for the first time, do not be discouraged; get up and try again. Keep bouncing back until you become successful. Let me narrate to you a true story: One day, as a child Thomas Alva Edison came home from school and gave a paper to his mother. He said to her, "Mom, my teacher gave this paper to me and told me only you are to read it. What does it say?" Her eyes welled with tears as she read the letter out loud to her child. "Your son is a genius. This school is too small for him and doesn't have good enough teachers to train him. Please teach him yourself." His mother did just that until she fell ill and passed away. Many years after Edison's mother died, he became one of the greatest inventors of the century. One day he was going through some of her things and found the folded letter that his old teacher wrote to his mother that day. He opened it. The message written in the letter was, "Your son is mentally deficient. We cannot let him attend our school anymore. He is expelled." Edison became emotional after reading it and then wrote in his diary: "Thomas A. Edison was a mentally deficient child whose mother turned him into the genius of the Century." Remember, people would more learn from their mistakes if they aren't so busy denying them. A positive word of encouragement can help someone achieve pinnacles in

life. So, no matter what happens in your life, **D**-O, not **D**-E-R-A-I-L, do not quit. The World has no place for a quitter.

Everything I have shared in the book is from the pages of my own life experiences. I dropped out of school in 1987. Eighteen years later, in 2005, it was tough for me to take the first step to go back to school, but once I took that step, two years later, I had my first bachelor's degree with a 3.93 GPA, and I kept going. In another two years, I completed my master's degree. There were times, I had a starving stomach, empty wallet, and a broken heart, but each time, I got up and bounced back. Remember, every person is a soldier by birth — either fighting for somebody else or fighting for himself or herself. If you give up, you would be a hundred percent failure, and you will be at the mercy of those whom you may not like much. On the other hand, if you keep fighting, there is a fifty percent chance you would be successful.

Let me recommend a practice that I follow holistically every day; each morning when you wake up, go in front of a mirror and practice saying at least ten times: "It's Easy, I Can Do It". Very soon, the word "Impossible" will disappear from your dictionary. "When you rise in life, your friends know who you are! When you fall, you know who your friends are." If you become successful, you will have plenty of followers. Be a leader, not a follower!

Acknowledgments

First, I would like to thank Hossein for sharing his life story with me. The last time when I spoke to Hossein on April 16, 2021, I came to know that his condition is now even worse than before. His salary is now reduced to 800 Dirham (around 218 USD). It was 900 Dirham (around 245 USD) before. Also, as the owner and his third wife live in the complex now, incidents of beating and abuse have increased. I asked him why the owner beat him, he replied, "For no reason.". He started crying. He also informed me that he is working only because of his family, especially for his daughter. She is sixteen now, and Hossein is fixing to get her married. I asked him she is still too young to get married and, it would be illegal because she is still a minor. However, Hossein sees no other way to improve his situation. He thinks that if she gets married, his burden would be less, and he may not have to work on the foreign land anymore.

I promised Hossein that I would try to help him in any lawful way I can. I encouraged him to hang tight for a few more months. That made Hossein emotional. With this book's proceedings, I intend to set up a charitable foundation to help Hossein and others like him. It does not take a lot to help these hard-working laborers who sacrifice their own happiness to benefit their family members. I hope Hossein's story gets accepted among the readers and touches the heart of many more people. I will believe that my hard work has borne fruit if even a single person gets benefited from this book.

While writing Hossein's story, I got lots of encouragement from my peers, friends, and family. Special thanks to Prof. Alamgir Toimoor and Mr. Anish Das Apu for this process. Initially, I was writing in bits and pieces; only for myself and close friends. But then, with their encouragement, I decided to compile all my stories and transform them into a book. Prof. Alamgir and Mr. Apu's argument is to let the world know about the stories of people like Hossein. They continuously inspired me wholeheartedly. As I have been living abroad for almost four decades, so Prof. Toimoor and Mr. Apu helped me edit the text and find a publisher in Bangladesh. With their support, I published my first book *"Attmoprokash (Self-revelation)"* in September 2020. The book is about my life during two years at Dhaka University as a student and some current burning issues.

Hossein's story was ongoing; so this book (Whispers and Wailings) was published in January 2021 in the Bengali version named *"Shonar Horinier Khoje"*. Many of my American friends and colleagues asked me to translate it into English so that they could read it. This triggered my sense of urgency to translate it. I must thank Dr. Andrew Boone, Col. James Cummings, and Col. Stephen Fabiano, who show continuous enthusiasm to read my book in English. It was because of their interest that I decided to translate it into English.

I thank my publisher, Happy Self Publishing, and my publishing consultants Jyotsna Ramachandran, Analie Aninon, Sushmitha Naroor, Nitin Dutta, and every person for their devoted work. Their wisdom, patience, and guidance have helped me polish and refine this book. I admire their episodes of Author Success Show.

Finally, I thank Prof. Saimun Afrojee for reading my story. I express my gratitude for her valued opinions, kindness, reading, re-reading, and helping me edit this book in the initial phase. English translation of Bengali poems and songs is not an easy task, and it's not a literal one, but it is an accepted translation by Prof. Afrojee. I am grateful to her for her earnest efforts.

Thank You

Thank You For Reading My Book!

I really appreciate all of your feedback, and I love hearing what you have to say.

I need your input to make the next version of this book and my future books even better.

Please leave me a helpful review on Amazon letting me know what you thought of the book.

Thank you so much!
Khan Mosleh

About Happy Self Publishing

Happy Self Publishing is a one-stop destination for online publishing services such as book cover design, editing, formatting, audiobook narration, website design, and marketing. At Happy Self Publishing we help authors find their voice and self-publish professionally.

▶ **WHAT WE DO:** We help coaches, consultants, trainers, speakers, and entrepreneurs who aspire to position themselves as the trusted experts in their field by helping them become bestselling authors within 6 months or less, even if they hate writing.

▶ **HOW WE DO IT:** We show you how to build a profitable author funnel and use the book as the lead magnet in the funnel to give you expert positioning and attract qualified leads for your business.

▶ **WHY IT WORKS:** After working with over 400 authors from 35 countries, we've been able to simplify the process and show you the easiest and fastest way to publish your book. It doesn't matter at what stage of your author journey you are currently - we have the tools & resources to take you to the next step and help you publish a world-class book.

▶ **SERVICES WE PROVIDE:**

- ✓ book writing aka angel writing
- ✓ editing
- ✓ book coaching
- ✓ book cover design
- ✓ formatting
- ✓ publishing ebooks, paperback & audiobooks
- ✓ author websites
- ✓ book trailers
- ✓ making it a #1 Amazon bestseller

Check us out on www.happyselfpublishing.com
YouTube: www.youtube.com/jyotsnaramachandran
Instagram: www.instagram.com/happyselfpub/
LinkedIn: www.linkedin.com/company/happyselfpublishing/mycompany/
Join our Happy Authors' Tribe:
www.facebook.com/groups/happyauthorstribe

www.ingramcontent.com/pod-product-compliance
Lightning Source LLC
Chambersburg PA
CBHW072151200426
43209CB00052B/1113